M

FROM WHERE I STAND

Flight #93 Pilot's Widow Sets the Record Straight

MELODIE HOMER

FROM WHERE I STAND

Flight #93 Pilot's Widow Sets the Record Straight

Langdon Street Press
Minneapolis, MN

Langdon Street Press
212 3rd Avenue North, Suite 290
Minneapolis, MN 55401
612.455.2293
www.langdonstreetpress.com

ISBN-13: 978-1-936782-74-1
LCCN: 2011943666

Distributed by Itasca Books

US Air Force Academy Photo by Denny Rogers
Cover Design by Deb Lengyl
Typeset by Melanie Shellito

Printed in the United States of America

To Laurel and Alden:

For finding your mother,
There's one certain test.
You must look for the creature
Who loves you the best.[1]

---

[1] *Little Miss Spider* by David Kirk

CONTENTS

FOREWORD

My name is Ellen Saracini. My husband, Captain Victor John Saracini, was the pilot of United Airlines Flight 175, which struck the south tower of the World Trade Center at 9:03 a.m. on September 11, 2001. I first met Melodie at LeRoy's memorial service. Her husband, First Officer LeRoy Homer, was killed when Flight 93 crashed in a field in Shanksville, Pennsylvania after it was hijacked by terrorists.

On September 11, Melodie and I shared a feeling that all control had been ripped from us. Within the first few hours we were dealing with United Airlines, the police, the FBI, and the media, never mind having to somehow tell our children what happened to their daddy. Within the next few weeks we were asked to take part in a wide variety of September 11 tributes, never giving us the time we needed to grieve. But hell has no fury like a woman whose life has been ripped apart. We became determined to fix the wrongs and to bring some semblance of control back into our lives.

Together we have traveled this new road while trying to make sense of senselessness.

As I read these pages about our numbing losses on September 11, I struggled with the trauma that took years to overcome. But reading the book also reminds me that good things can come out of even the worst circumstances. One of the outcomes of our tragedy and grief is that we have the opportunity to honor the lives of our husbands and carry on their names.

As traumatic as that day was for America and for the families of the murdered, when the dust settled, we were able to create a bond of friendship that transcends the grief. My friendship with Melodie is precious. There is nothing I could say to her that she would not understand, accept, and support. I have told Melodie, "I hate that I ever met you, and yet I'm so glad that I did."

This book is not for the faint of heart. The magnitude of pain and suffering that we endured is presented in an unvarnished manner. The book serves as a reminder that we must never forget our vulnerability. The world has changed forever. The battlefield of war now encompasses every possible place that humanity touches. Read the book to experience a national tragedy. Read the book to remember.

— Ellen Saracini, 2011

INTRODUCTION

September 11, 2001 isn't on people's minds as it once was. I have watched people who lost loved ones find happiness again. But for many, including me, it is still a struggle ten years later. I suppose I thought that eventually life would return to some sort of normal. This notion was completely inaccurate. Strangers recognize me on the street from seeing my picture in the paper or from watching an interview on television. There have been numerous times my phone has rung with the media wanting to know my opinion on various new stories: airport security measures, the treatment of detainees at Guantanamo Bay, thwarted terrorist attacks, and most recently, the killing of Osama bin Laden. Eventually I realized I had no choice but to accept this new normal—life after September 11, 2001.

My husband was the first officer on board United Airlines Flight 93 when it crashed in Shanksville, Pennsylvania on that Tuesday morning. Over time I realized there were so many misconceptions about what happened not only on that flight but after September 11, 2001, and I wanted to make those right.

This book chronicles my life over the past decade. I have raised my daughter on my own since she was ten months old, and then made the decision to adopt another child, my son, in 2004. I have struggled with post-traumatic stress disorder (PTSD). I have had conflicts with my husband's employer, United Airlines. I have felt betrayal by many people, including people I had considered to be my friends. I became disillusioned with the country which had become my home over the past twenty years, an administration that had not been able to protect my husband.

This is not the first book to be written about Flight 93 and probably will not be the last. However, it is truthful. For example, most people are still unaware that the pilots on board Flight 93 were not immediately killed by the hijackers. My husband, LeRoy, and Captain Jason Dahl both played a part in diverting the aircraft into a deserted field in western Pennsylvania, away from the U.S. Capitol.

* * *

I was watching television on the evening of Sunday, May 1, 2011 when the program was interrupted by the news that Osama bin Laden was dead. Stunned, I listened to the president as he described how the mastermind of the September 11 attacks had been tracked and killed. I had rarely thought about this evil man over the past decade, and had made my peace with the fact that he would eventually grow old and die in a cave somewhere in the Middle East.

Within minutes of hearing the news of bin Laden's death, the media frenzy began all over again. I experienced feelings reminiscent of the days immediately following September 11; I was trying to absorb information while being pursued by the media, who within five minutes of the president's special report were calling me at home, wanting to know my reaction. It took some time to get over the shock and consider my feelings. And when I did finally agree to be interviewed, all I could say was that a dangerous, evil man had been killed; the world would be safer now that he was gone. Although the death of bin Laden was a victory for many Americans who watched the towers fall that day, bin Laden's death provided no closure for me. But I had never expected that it would. I didn't wake up in the morning and go to bed at night wondering when Osama bin Laden would be captured. In fact, he was not someone I thought about very much at all.

I was fortunate enough to be one of about sixty people to meet with President Obama in New York on May 8, 2011. He told us that even though he knew Osama bin Laden's death didn't change anything in regards to the loss of our loved ones, he wanted us to know that we were never forgotten. When I decided to write this book, I wanted to share my experience of living in the aftermath of September 11, and to correct the misinformation about LeRoy that had developed over the years. I want people to know who LeRoy was and how he affected the course of that day. I want a written record that honors LeRoy and his legacy, for me, our family, and the world. My hope is that people will understand that part of the difficulty with moving on from an event like this is that as much as we would prefer to forget, that day is ever present.

1

OUR LIFE BEFORE

"The life of the dead is placed in the memory of the living."

—Marcus T. Cicero

For me this sequence of events began in November of 2000. Of course I realized this only in retrospect, "after everything happened." This was how I now defined time. "Before everything happened" and "after everything happened" were the only distinctions that mattered, the time before and after LeRoy was no longer with me.

I remember a November night when my husband and I were watching the election results come in. We eventually went to sleep, thinking, as I'm sure a lot of people did, that Al Gore would be the next president of the United States. When we woke up, we were both shocked to find that George W. Bush had won. Looking back, this was the moment when the course of my life was irreversibly altered.

November 2000 was a great time in our lives. LeRoy and I had been married for two years, and our daughter Laurel had been born a few weeks earlier in late October. We were captivated by our sweet little baby and relished our role as parents. As we adjusted to our new routines, we were tired but content. The post-election controversy wore on, and we were aware of the court rulings and ballot recounts in Florida, but we were too happily wrapped up in our own lives to pay these developments much attention.

LeRoy and I had met five years earlier in a movie-of-the-week kind of way. I had been living in Southern California, working as a nurse and attending graduate school. One of the nurses I had previously worked with had relocated to New Jersey when her husband, an Air Force pilot, was transferred to McGuire Air Force Base. LeRoy was also an Air Force pilot stationed at McGuire. Eventually our mutual friends decided that—despite the distance and without any idea if we would have any chemistry—we should meet.

LeRoy called me on August 16, 1995, the same day he got my phone number. Our first phone call lasted for over an hour. We talked about our families, our careers, what we enjoyed doing in our free time—the usual getting-to-know-you conversation topics. When LeRoy mentioned he was turning thirty that month, we discovered our birthdays were a year and two days apart.

LeRoy had been hired as a pilot by United Airlines that May after serving in the U.S. Air Force for seven years and flying the C-141 Starlifter. He lived in Marlton, a small town in southern New Jersey, and a short commute to McGuire Air Force Base where he had been stationed during his active service. He told me a little bit about his family. He had been born and raised on Long Island, New York in a biracial home with his German mother and African-American father. His parents had met when his dad was in the Army and stationed in Germany. His dad had passed away when he was twelve years old, so his mom had raised him and his three siblings by herself.

During this initial call, I told him a bit about my upbringing, too. My parents had emigrated from Jamaica to Canada in the '60s. My two siblings and I were all born and raised in southern Ontario. I had made the move to California in the fall of 1989 to go back to school for my bachelor's degree in nursing. At this point, I had already completed a community college nursing program and had worked as a registered nurse on an orthopedic surgical floor for a couple of years. I had completed my master's degree in nursing the month before LeRoy had called for the first time and planned on staying in California for another year at most, before I started looking for a position as a clinical nurse educator—the focus of my graduate work. It was easy to talk to LeRoy, and the connection I felt to this person I had never even seen was immediate.

The reason I remember the date of our first conversation is because I was leaving to go to Europe the next day as a graduation present to myself. LeRoy had taken a similar backpacking vacation after he had graduated from the Air Force Academy and had lots of advice for me. I had planned to travel with a suitcase. But somehow he managed to talk me into using a backpack instead. I don't take advice easily, especially if I don't know someone. But of course he was right. I would have been miserable trying to maneuver a suitcase on trains and buses, and would have had difficulty trying to roll a suitcase through many of the streets in France, Italy, and England—the countries I visited on the trip.

Even though I really enjoyed the telephone conversation with LeRoy, I was determined to put him out of my mind. I was going to be out of the country for a month. A lot could happen in four weeks and I had no idea if I would hear from him again once I returned. After all, it was one phone call with a person I had never met—a person who lived 3000 miles away. I told him the date that I would be returning to California and that we would talk again then. But I was still not sure we would reconnect. I would be gone for almost a month. I wasn't so sure he would be waiting when I got back. I started to feel a little more hopeful when I called my answering machine towards the end of my trip. LeRoy had remembered my birthday and had left me a message wishing me a happy day and telling me that he looked forward to talking to me when I got back.

When I returned to California in September, I waited for a phone call. But LeRoy didn't call. I was disappointed but not surprised. After all, this was why I had put any thoughts of him out of my mind. A couple of weeks went by. One night while at work, I was telling a fellow nurse how I had never heard back from LeRoy. She urged me to call him. What did I have to lose? I finally took her advice and called him. It turns out I had promised to call *him* when I got back from Europe; in my determination to put him out of my mind while I was away, I had forgotten this part of the conversation. Here he thought I had blown him off.

After a few weeks of daily two- and three-hour phone calls, LeRoy told me he would be coming out to California to visit for the weekend. He announced this without giving me a chance to think about it. He had simply decided it was time for us to meet face to face. Being a romantic at heart, and possibly a bit crazy, I went to pick LeRoy up at LAX Airport, not even sure I would recognize him. I still remember the apprehension

I felt driving the hour and a half from where I lived in San Bernardino to Los Angeles. I already knew that I was starting to care for this person with whom I had spoken every day. But what if he wasn't the same person I had already grown fond of? I knew I'd be crushed.

When we had originally made arrangements to meet at the airport, I asked LeRoy how I would be able to recognize him. He told me he would be wearing his United Airlines uniform. All I knew about LeRoy's physical appearance was that he was a thirty-year-old man with light brown skin that reflected his biracial background.

I knew him as soon as I saw him. Even before he said a word, I felt relieved. I knew instantly he was the same person I had grown to care about during the many hours we had spent talking to each other. I knew from looking into the warmth of his eyes that my decision to meet him in person was going to be okay. My heart was happy.

We had a great weekend spending time together and getting to know each other. I took LeRoy to some of my favorite local places. We drove up to Lake Arrowhead and had breakfast at a Belgian waffle restaurant. Then that evening we walked around Old Town Pasadena, having dinner at one of the local restaurants. There were no awkward pauses in conversation; in fact, we had so much to talk about. The hours we had spent talking over the phone made our time together comfortable. It felt like we had known each other for years. At the end of the weekend LeRoy told me he wanted to pursue a relationship with me. "I don't see distance being an issue," he said. He would simply arrange his schedule so he could fly more trips to California. His suggestion amazed me. I had never been with someone so focused and direct.

LeRoy was true to his word. He flew to California at least once a month—sometimes once a week—over the next few months. Since I worked twelve-hour shifts, I was able to adjust my schedule to coincide with his, and I would drive out to Los Angeles to meet him at the airport. If he had a few days off, he would fly to California as a passenger and spend them with me. I made a couple of trips out to New Jersey as well. By December, LeRoy had started to nonchalantly insert the phrase "when you move to New Jersey" into our conversations. If I was complaining about something that had happened at work, well, I didn't need to worry about it much longer because I would be moving to New Jersey. I had never felt this secure in a relationship before and we had only met for the first time face to face a month earlier. I had never planned to live in California indefinitely; now that I had completed my education, I was prepared to move back to Canada since all my friends and family were there.

Instead, I relocated to New Jersey in July 1996. LeRoy proposed on Valentine's Day the following year, two years after our initial phone call; we were married on May 24, 1998. Several months into our relationship he confided that he knew he was going to marry me the first weekend he came to meet me.

We knew we both wanted kids, but we also wanted to spend time together, just the two of us, before we started a family. We took trips to Greece and Germany and went on a Caribbean cruise in the first years we were married. I had transitioned from working as a staff nurse to a position as a nurse consultant for a pharmaceutical company in 1997, which allowed me flexibility in my schedule. I worked out of my home office and provided educational programs to physicians' offices and hospitals in the Philadelphia area. I also helped run patient education fairs and support groups. Although my participation in these programs was coordinated by Ortho Biotech's sales representatives, I made my own schedule which allowed me to take advantage of a huge perk: as the spouse of an airline employee, I could fly on LeRoy's flights for free as long as there was an empty seat on the plane.

LeRoy flew the New York-London route a lot and I went with him enough times that I knew the flight attendants and the desk staff at the London layover hotel by name. During the two- or three-day layovers, we would squeeze in as many activities as we could: high tea at the Lanesborough Hotel, walks in Hyde Park, shopping at Harrods. On one of his London trips I took LeRoy to see *The Importance of Being Earnest,* a play I had seen on my trip to Europe several years earlier. My own job required I travel a few times a year for work-related meetings, and LeRoy would coordinate his schedule so he could come with me. While I went to meetings during the day, he would explore the local museums or read by the pool. I would meet him at lunch and at dinner. Over time the people I worked with got to know LeRoy and seemed to enjoy having him around. LeRoy had the ability to talk to anyone he met, always genuinely interested in other people regardless of whether he had anything in common with them.

Shortly after we met, LeRoy had been promoted from second officer on the Boeing 727 to a first officer on the Boeing 757 and 767. From February to April 1996, he trained at United Airlines' training center in Denver. Usually a pilot is trained to fly only one type of aircraft at a time, but these two airplanes were so similar that pilots were trained to fly both. Aside from his training, LeRoy worked about fourteen days a month, and he was usually gone for two or three days at a time. When he was away on a trip we would talk at least once a day.

When his plane landed back in New York at the end of the trip, he would call to tell me he was on the ground and would be home in a couple of hours.

When I think about our life together, and how we chose to live it, it was almost like LeRoy knew he wouldn't be here for a long time. LeRoy was the anti-couch potato; Wimbledon and the U.S. Open were the only sports he watched on television. Instead, when LeRoy was home, we went on picnics, visited the local museums, and took road trips around New Jersey and Pennsylvania. One of our favorite things to do was drive into New York City for dinner and a show. When we were home, we read in front of a warm fire, or sat out on our porch, listening to music and watching the sky. I have a wonderful memory of us sitting on the porch during a storm, cuddled together under a blanket on the wicker couch, just watching the rain.

* * *

LeRoy had begun the habit of printing me a copy of his schedule when I was living in California, so I would be able to call him if I needed to. Flight numbers, take-off and landing times, names of layover hotels, and the hotel phone numbers were also printed on the schedule. LeRoy's schedule changed every month. He would enter the criteria he wanted for the following month into United's WinBid computer program: his preferred days off, and his choice of airports and destinations. Once this information was entered, lists of possible schedules, or "lines" as the pilots refer to them, were displayed. From these lines, LeRoy would select his preferred line, followed by his second choice and so on. Then the computer would assign his final schedule based on date-of-hire seniority. LeRoy would usually try to find lines with weekends off, and with departures out of Kennedy or Newark. United pilots based in New York flew trips out of all three local airports—Kennedy, Newark, and LaGuardia—but LeRoy tried to avoid trips flying out of LaGuardia because take-off times were usually very early in the morning and we lived about two and a half hours away. Most of the time LeRoy would get one of his top choices; he had been with United since 1995 and had built up some seniority. He liked to fly the "trans cons"—the coast-to-coast New York to Los Angeles or San Francisco trips—as well as flights from New York to London. He loved spending his layovers in large urban cities with museums, great restaurants, and outdoor spaces where he could rollerblade or jog to stay in shape while on the road.

I missed LeRoy when he was away, but I was fine on my own. I kept myself busy with work and household chores, and, after our baby was born in October 2000, looking after her occupied much of my time. Besides, LeRoy was always a phone call away. The anticipation of his return home was a constant, and always made me feel better. His schedule did vary from month to month, but the upside to having him be away for three or four days was that when he was home, we could spend whole days together. I tried to arrange my work schedule so that we could make up the time together during the week, which made up for the fifteen days a month he was away. We would go to lunch or drive over the bridge into Philadelphia and visit the Museum of Art. We could go see a matinee in the middle of the day or spend time on Long Beach Island. It was wonderful having him home. Even if we were just doing errands, LeRoy wanted us to do them together. Once, I suggested we split the list, and do our errands separately to save time. LeRoy wasn't having that. Even if it took us twice the time, he wanted to spend the time together.

When I was pregnant with Laurel, I told LeRoy I wanted to wait until the baby was born to have a family baby shower. Since we had decided not to find out the gender, having the shower after the baby came would not only allow everyone to meet the baby, but also to know whether to come bearing pink or blue gifts. My mom came from Canada to be there for Laurel's birth and to help me when I came home from the hospital when LeRoy went back to work. One day, LeRoy suggested we take my mom out for Sunday brunch, even though Laurel was just a week and a half old. As we were getting ready to leave the quaint French restaurant, LeRoy left to go to the bathroom. It seemed he was gone for a long time, and I was getting irritated because I was ready to leave. After he returned to the table, several more minutes passed before the waitress brought us our check. When we left the restaurant, LeRoy suddenly remembered he needed to get gas. By this time I was really getting annoyed. I wanted to get the baby home because she needed a clean diaper; there had been no changing table in the restaurant's bathroom. After we gassed up, LeRoy turned the wrong direction out of the gas station. I was practically breathing fire.

When we were finally headed in the right direction towards home, he reminded me he had to drop off some information on the U.S. Air Force Academy to my girlfriend, Stephanie, because her nephew was interested in attending the Academy. I had overheard him on the phone earlier in the morning before we left for the restaurant telling Stephanie he would drop off some information. By now I had really had it. I was cranky and I just wanted to go home. I told LeRoy that the rest of us would wait in the car while he dropped off the information.

When we got to Stephanie's house, my mom

jumped out of the car and said she needed to use the bathroom. Hello? Hadn't I just said no one was to get out of the car? Hadn't we just left a very nice restaurant with an equally nice restroom? Then Stephanie came out to the car, and took Laurel out of her car seat, saying I should come in for just a minute. I argued and fussed all the way to her front door, down her stairs, and right into my surprise baby shower. With lots of help from Stephanie, LeRoy had actually planned my baby shower. My friends and coworkers were there, as well as some friends from out of town whom I hadn't seen in ages. All of the women in LeRoy's family were there, too. LeRoy stayed for the entire shower and took pictures, completely unconcerned that he was the only guy there. This was the guy I had fallen in love with.

In December 2000, as we were writing our Christmas cards, we decided to make an early New Year's resolution. Instead of writing "hope to see you this year," we resolved that we would actually do it. We were going to be housebound with the baby, and I liked to cook, so we decided we would invite people over for dinner more often. And we did. We continued to travel, just a bit less than before. Laurel's first trip was to Canada when she was eight weeks old. Sticking to our New Year's resolution, I looked up an old friend when we were in San Francisco in January 2001, who I hadn't seen in years, and we all went to dinner—LeRoy and I with the baby in the stroller, and my friend, Ruby, and her husband, Tom.

LeRoy had vacation days in April and wanted to go away for a few days. We flew my mom in to watch Laurel and went to Cancun. On the flight to Mexico, I felt sad being away from my baby for the first time since she was born. I was even a bit irritable with LeRoy for making me leave her. To give me a distraction, we made two lists of places we wanted to visit. One list was made up of places we wanted to travel with kids; the second was places we wanted to visit just the two of us. We wrote the list on a blank page of the Cancun guidebook we had with us. I keep the guide in my bookcase, and refer to it once in a while when I'm planning family vacations.

In May we took Laurel to Southern California. We both had friends out there and we wanted them to meet her. June was LeRoy's first Father's Day and we celebrated by taking him to a nice brunch in Philadelphia. We spent a lot more time with family and friends that summer. We were in Canada in July so I could be at the birth of my best friend Pam's third baby. After my week in Chicago for work, we went to Long Island and spent time with LeRoy's high school friends. At the end of July we attended LeRoy's sister Cheryl's fiftieth birthday party, spending time with LeRoy's entire family.

In August 2001, I surprised LeRoy for his birthday with concert tickets to see Sade in concert. He had never been to a live concert before and was so excited. It was an incredible show and one of those memories that is always with me. A song by Sade brings me back to that night and the love we had for each other.

August was also when we took Laurel to the beach for the first time. I remember how funny she was, looking at the sand and then purposely taking a header right into it. I think she wanted to know what it felt like. We had dinner celebrating LeRoy's birthday at one of his favorite restaurants before leaving the next day to spend Labor Day in Canada.

Labor Day weekend was perfect. My whole family was at my parent's house for lunch. We were discussing when and where the next family vacation would be. Laurel was starting to stand and hold onto things and she was slowly making her way around the coffee table in my parents' living room. I remember feeling like this was a picture perfect moment. We flew back to New Jersey on Labor Day and headed up to North Jersey for a barbecue with LeRoy's friends and coworkers. When I reflect back on how we spent those last few months, I have no regrets. We lived our entire time together in a way that makes me proud.

When I was thirty two weeks pregnant with Laurel, I managed to sneak one last vacation in with LeRoy on one of his work trips. I couldn't have known that this would be the last time I would ever fly on an airplane piloted by LeRoy. I had always wanted my parents to have the opportunity to fly with LeRoy as their pilot, so in August 2000, my parents and I flew with him to London to celebrate my thirty-fourth birthday. My parents were thrilled to have the experience, and we spent three days there. We showed my parents around, and took them to the places we had loved on our previous visits. The Notting Hill Carnival was going on at the time, so we walked through the streets, enjoying the music and the food. During one of our previous trips, LeRoy and I had found a Thai restaurant we really liked and we took my parents there for my birthday dinner. Two months later, Laurel was born; two weeks later, there was an election.

2

THE DAY

"Lost but never gone,
Missed but never forgotten.
Living on through those who will always remember
Our brothers, heroes of the sky."

—Megan Seal

My communications with United Airlines started shortly after 9:00 a.m. on September 11, 2001. I had taken Laurel across the street to my neighbor Digna's house as per our morning routine, and was contemplating going to the gym. I turned on the TV and was walking back into the kitchen to make my breakfast when I saw an airplane hit a building. What was I watching?

I walked back into the family room towards the television and tried to make sense of the images. I didn't know it at the time, but what I had seen was

United Airlines Flight 175 crashing into the South Tower of the World Trade Center. This was the first but not the last instance during the grueling course of the day when I would have no idea how much time had gone by.

LeRoy had left earlier that morning for his flight out of Newark to San Francisco. I had heard the alarm, the sounds of him getting up and taking a shower. He always assembled his uniform so that he wouldn't have to turn on any lights when he left in the morning. I heard the shower turn on but fell asleep again. He came around to my side of the bed to let me know he was leaving, that he would call when he landed, and that he loved me.

One of the first things I remember hearing as I stared at my television screen was a newscaster saying, in an attempt to make sense of what was happening, that maybe there was some sort of air traffic control problem. Evidently a small plane had already hit the other tower of the World Trade Center.

It didn't matter what the problem was—fear had already started to creep into my body. I called the United Airlines flight office at Kennedy Airport and spoke with a receptionist at the front desk. Even though I knew LeRoy's flight had left from Newark, flight operations for all three New York area airports took place at the Kennedy flight office. I explained who I was and gave the receptionist LeRoy's flight number, Flight 93. She put me on hold, and when she came back on the line a few minutes later, she reassured me he was fine. "I promise you, everything is okay." Those words would echo in my mind for years.

She asked me if I wanted to send a message to the cockpit for LeRoy. I knew about the computer in the cockpit, called ACARS (Aircraft Communication Addressing and Recording System), which received messages from the New York flight center. LeRoy had pointed it out to me on one of my preflight visits to the cockpit. At this point, I was sobbing uncontrollably from the relief of knowing he was okay. I took a couple of breaths and with my voice still cracking, I asked her to send a message. The message she typed for me said: "Just wanted to make sure you are okay."

My neighbor had come over earlier in the morning and had been there when United had told me everything was all right with LeRoy's flight. But shortly afterwards, the announcement was made that the local schools were closing and parents needed to pick up their children, so she left to go pick up her kids. I had been fielding calls from family and friends all morning, most of which are a blur, but I remember talking to Joe at least twice before he called for the last time. Joe was a friend of LeRoy's who had flown C-141s with him during their time at McGuire Air Force Base.

LeRoy had a group of friends who he had met through McGuire: Steve Scheri, Marty Hnatov, Mark Ulrich, and Joe "Mak" Maksimczyk. When their active duty with the U.S. Air Force was complete, they had all made the transition to commercial flying, and all of them had been hired by United, flying out of a New York pilot domicile. All except for Joe, who decided to move out west. Even after Joe left the area, they remained close; Joe and Marty were groomsmen at our wedding. Now working for United Airlines and based out of LAX in California, Joe had access to United Airlines' "Apollo"—the airline's private computer system—and was able to track LeRoy's flight; he had been calling periodically to give me updates.

Once CNN announced the decision had been made to ground all planes, I called United's New York flight office for the second time to find out where LeRoy's flight would be landing. They told me he would complete his flight and land in San Francisco as planned. This didn't make sense to me. According to his schedule, he wasn't supposed to land for a couple more hours. If all planes were being told to land, why wouldn't he be landing in, say, Denver?

With all this in my head when Joe called that last time around 11:00 a.m., I was sure he was calling to tell me where LeRoy would be landing. Maybe the information on Apollo was more accurate than the information the New York flight office had given me. I didn't even catch on when he asked me if I was by myself. Yes, I was by myself. Had he found anything out?

I already knew from watching CNN that two other planes had crashed—one at the Pentagon and one in Pennsylvania. But I knew from the schedule that LeRoy's flight, Flight 93, had taken off at 8:00 a.m., so neither of those flights could have been his. The plane at the Pentagon was identified pretty quickly as an American Airlines flight, but the plane in Pennsylvania had not yet been identified by airline or number. I was relieved because I knew it couldn't be LeRoy's plane. Flight 93 was headed to San Francisco, and would be nowhere near Pennsylvania. With an 8:00 a.m. takeoff, it would be safely in the Midwest by now.

But then Joe told me: the plane that had crashed in Pennsylvania was LeRoy's. I remember hearing Joe say those words. *This isn't happening, this isn't happening,* my mind was telling me. I was pounding on my kitchen window with my open hand, pounding as hard as I could, screaming at Joe, "Take it back! Take it back!" But then abruptly, somehow, I managed to calm myself down. I told Joe it wasn't true. Joe had seen LeRoy's flight number on CNN. But I was also watching CNN and they had not released any flight numbers.

There had been misinformation all morning. The report that a small plane had hit the World Trade

Center was wrong; in fact, it turned out to be a wide-body commercial jetliner. Then one of the morning shows had mentioned that maybe there were air traffic control problems in the New York area. Flights were being confused, and no one seemed to know what was really going on. It had to be a West Coast technical thing that had led to CNN's inconsistent broadcasting.

I had no idea that LeRoy's plane, Flight 93, had not actually taken off at 8:00 a.m. Because of heavy airplane traffic on the tarmac, LeRoy's flight had pushed back from the gate on time, but did not take off until 8:42 a.m. Joe wanted me to stay on the phone with him, but I had to go pick up Laurel. I suddenly needed her to be with me. As I crossed the street to Digna's house, our mailman, Chuck, was driving towards me. He stopped his truck and asked me where LeRoy was. Chuck and LeRoy had gotten to know each other in the nine years LeRoy had been living there, and would often chat about travel. I told Chuck that LeRoy was flying, but that I had talked to United and he was okay. I continued on to Digna's house. When I got there, I told her I didn't want to be alone, so I picked up Laurel and brought her back home.

Back in my own house, I sat down in front of the television again. It couldn't have been more than five minutes before CNN aired footage of the Pennsylvania crash site. LeRoy's flight number, the flight number from his schedule taped to the refrigerator, was at the bottom of the screen. Flight 93. I screamed.

I couldn't find the numbers on the phone fast enough. I called Digna. "You have to come get her." I was already on the phone with the flight office when Digna ran in, scooped Laurel up, and ran out.

I tried to keep the hysteria out of my voice. I explained how I had just been watching CNN and had seen LeRoy's flight number on the screen. "You *promised* me everything was all right!"

The person who answered the phone said, "Someone will have to call you back."

I'm not sure how long it took for Bob Spielman, the chief pilot, to call me back, but it seemed like too long. The chief pilot is the individual who is responsible for the supervision of the flight and ground crew in flight operations. Bob Spielman was the chief pilot for the New York area. His job was a supervisory one in addition to performing the duties of a captain when flying. I don't know for sure who he had to speak with that day, but he did speak with all of the pilots' families and was our initial source of communication with United. My conversation with Bob was brief. He confirmed it was LeRoy's flight. He sounded distraught as he told me he believed there had been possibly a dozen attempted hijackings at United that day. "But I called and you said he was all right," I repeated. Bob told me there were likely no survivors from the crash. I hung up. My conversation with him is the last clear sense of time I had for the rest of the day.

The phone rang all morning. I watched the number of messages go up number by number until it was in the double digits. The messages were pretty much the same; the caller was sure LeRoy was okay but with everything they had seen on TV, they wanted to call and check.

Now I had to call LeRoy's family and my own and tell them that the unimaginable had happened. First, I called my dad and my brother. The border crossing between the United States and Canada had closed as a result of the attacks, so it would be a couple of days before they could get to me. My mom and a friend from church were on an Alaskan cruise at the time. My mom had been watching television while she was getting ready for breakfast on the ship and saw the plane hit the South Tower. She had heard planes were being grounded and assumed LeRoy was in Europe and would be stranded. When she called, she asked me where LeRoy was. And I told her LeRoy's plane had crashed. My mom started screaming and the line went dead. It would be several hours before I talked with her again; she had had to be sedated by the ship's physician.

As out of my mind as I was, I feared telling my sister the most. In 1996, Heather's best friend had died suddenly from complications of sickle cell anemia. Heather went into a deep depression, withdrawing completely from everyone. It had taken two years for her to return to her old self again. When it came to LeRoy, he and Heather had developed a good relationship. When she called our house, it wasn't just to talk to me, but to LeRoy, too. Heather talked to LeRoy about everything that was going on in her life—guys she was dating, frustrations with her job, whatever was on her mind. I was afraid Heather would not be able to take another sudden loss; I couldn't bear to lose her, too.

I called Heather's office and asked for her supervisor. I told her what had happened and asked if she could tell my sister, so that Heather wouldn't be alone when she heard. Heather's husband, her boyfriend at the time, worked at the same place, so I asked her supervisor to tell them together.

I also feared telling my mother-in-law, Ilse, the news, but knew I had to. I didn't want her to find out about LeRoy on TV the way I had. LeRoy and his mom were quite close, and I feared what might happen if she was alone when she found out LeRoy's plane had gone down. Cell phones weren't working in New York and it was several hours before I was able to get through to one of LeRoy's sisters. Monique worked nights but had called me right after I had spoken to United the first time and I told her everything was fine. So she had gone to sleep. When I was finally able to get through to her again, I heard her screaming to whoever was in the room, "It was LeRoy's plane." We didn't speak long because I told her someone needed to get to her mom before she saw it on the news. Monique was able to get in touch with one of LeRoy's other sisters who lived close to where my mother-in-law was living in Queens; she was able to tell her in person. I have a memory of speaking with my mother-in-law after she heard. She was crying and repeating "Why LeRoy?" and "What are we going to do?" over and over again. I did feel a sense of relief after our conversation, though. The calls had been made. I had done my job.

Later in the afternoon, Marty and Steve arrived. Joe had called them and told them it was LeRoy's plane. A little while later, Mark came by. My friend Stephanie came over. Everyone took turns answering the phone because I didn't want to talk to anyone. Someone started calling LeRoy's friends and contacts in his address book to let them know what had happened. It was early evening when a call came from someone at United suggesting that I leave my house as soon as possible. Apparently, the media would find out where I lived very quickly, and if I didn't want to deal with the inevitable chaos, I needed to stay somewhere else. Unfortunately, the one place where I wanted to be—at home with my family in Canada—was not a possibility because the border crossing had been closed given the security concerns. Even if the border crossing had been open, I don't think I would have been able to get myself to Canada, or anywhere else for that matter. I was emotionally and physically incapacitated and decided to stay home.

Our house backed up to woods, so we had never bothered to get blinds for the windows in the rear. My friends who were there covered the windows with sheets as a precaution. Digna brought Laurel home. When the media showed up, the township police set up a blockade at the entrance of our cul-de-sac. Several reporters walked up to the house on foot. Regardless, they never saw me. I was in bed for almost a week.

3

THE DAY AFTER

"For everything there is a season,
And a time for every matter under heaven:
A time to be born, and a time to die."

—Ecclesiastes 3:1

Every time I woke up, I would remember. This happened over and over again that first night. A deeper state of sleep allowed me to forget, until a dream or some sixth sense would rouse me. I was allowed a few seconds of calm before I would remember. Then I would scream, cry, claw at my clothes. "I can't do this," I yelled out. I would eventually fall back asleep, only to wake up and repeat the cycle again.

The comings and goings of family, friends, and neighbors continued for several days. I could hear all the activity from my bedroom. The phone rang incessantly. United had assigned Marty and Steve to stay with me to be a single point of contact from the company. They took turns staying at my home and helped with everything from paperwork to making sure we were protected from the media. Steve and Marty assisted in getting travel arrangements made for the memorials; supported us until the crisis management team arrived; dealt with the various agencies, like the FBI, who needed DNA samples; they even arranged to have LeRoy's car driven back to New Jersey from the employee parking lot. They made sure that the Air Line Pilots Association (ALPA) was involved from the beginning so that I had the representation I needed during a time when it was difficult to advocate for myself. All four of the pilots' wives were assigned pilots to assist them; luckily in my case, these were individuals I already knew. I had known both Steve and Marty for almost as long as I had known LeRoy.

My sister-in-law Cheryl was the first person from LeRoy's family to arrive, and even though she had just driven from Virginia, she immediately went grocery shopping. I remember she was wearing a fanny pack. It all seemed so strange—the fanny pack, the grocery shopping. She came back with all this food, and I had no idea who would be eating it. She bought Twinkies. I don't eat Twinkies. She bought single-ply toilet paper. I remember thinking that maybe when all the things that didn't belong in my house were gone—the toilet paper, the Twinkies, the extra large boxes of tissue—everything would go back to normal.

No one close to me had ever died before, and I never anticipated how many people would show up; some came for a few hours and others stayed for days. The border crossing reopened on September 12, and my dad, brother, and sister-in-law were able to arrive soon after; my mom was still stuck in Alaska. LeRoy's mom, his seven sisters, and a brother I had never met all came into town. They spent the days at my house, and the nights at a nearby hotel, but I stayed in bed most of the time. I hadn't invited anyone here, so why should I have to entertain them? I stopped eating and drinking and bathing. When someone forced me to eat, the food went right through me. I lost ten pounds that first week.

Early on, Johnson & Johnson's head office had called to offer me mental health support through their Employee Assistance Program (EAP). I had been working as a nurse consultant with a Johnson & Johnson company at the time, and was not technically eligible for the services because I was not an employee. However, my clients were extremely concerned and wanted to help me out in any way they could. United Airlines had indicated a crisis team was on its way to provide crisis counseling, but since no one had any idea when this was going to happen, I accepted the offer from Johnson & Johnson.

I can't recall the name of the counselor who called my home from EAP; I can't even remember much of what she said. But when someone says the wrong thing, you remember. So when the counselor said she knew how I felt because her husband had divorced her, I was completely taken aback. I wanted to scream, *your husband did not die without giving you the opportunity to say goodbye. You did not have to see his name scrolling across the bottom of the television screen over and over and over again.* But instead I said very little and ended the call. I never spoke with her again.

In those first days, the daylight seemed easier to bear than the dark of night. I lay in the quiet. With my bedroom door closed, the muffled voices of family were the only sounds I heard. I would pull out one of LeRoy's shirts and breathe it in. The smell of him was comforting. I would have moments when I would sob uncontrollably, unable to hold in the intense pain. But all the activity around me, even though I wasn't really a part of it, was at least a numbing distraction.

Our daughter Laurel spent the days at Digna's house. I didn't feel capable of taking care of her, and I didn't want her to be in the house with all the disruptions. I wanted her daily routine to remain the same. I'm not sure how she got to Digna's or who brought her home in the evenings. I don't know if I dressed her or gave her baths. For the first few days, I didn't even want to see her. It was too painful. Laurel was an innocent baby, a beautiful little girl. She had done nothing wrong, and yet she would never grow up with her dad.

At times I would tell myself it was all a mistake. Yes, the plane had crashed. But I knew LeRoy could survive this. They just hadn't found him yet. I would secretly call his cell phone repeatedly over the next few weeks when no one was around. There was a small part of me that hoped he would answer, that he was hurt and hadn't been found or that none of what they were telling me was real. But as I watched the images from the crash site on TV, the reality that LeRoy was not coming home slowly began to sink in. I no longer had those few precious seconds of Not Knowing when I woke up—I now woke up to the same nightmare I had just left in my sleep. I would run out to the garage when these constant and unbearable dreams occurred because I didn't want my screams to wake Laurel. I became fearful of falling asleep.

LeRoy usually carried his Swiss Army knife with him on his trips. I think it was the military side of him—always prepared whether he needed nail clippers or a corkscrew. He had two suitcases for work—the bigger bag was for international trips, the smaller one for domestic trips. On the night of September 12 as I was lying awake, I remembered the knife and jumped out of bed to look for it. I knew if I didn't find it, it meant he would have had it with him, which meant he could have had a way to defend himself. I found the knife in his international suitcase. He had taken the smaller suitcase when he left for San Francisco on September 11, because he would only be gone for one night.

I often wondered what would have happened if he had taken the other suitcase, the one with the knife. Would he have been able to use it to defend himself and the airplane? The question always in the forefront of my mind was, *Why? Why me and why LeRoy?* I waited for a loud voice, God's voice, to come out of the sky. My faith in God remained as it had always been. I understood that bad things happen; after all, humans have free will and evil exists in the world as a result. But I knew there was a reason this had happened to LeRoy, to me, and to our family. I just wanted—needed—to know what that reason was.

It seemed there was nothing I could do to distract myself from the pain. When the activity around me stopped at the end of the day, the numbness would lift, and I would feel like I was drowning. I tried to distract myself. I wrote thank-you cards to the people who had sent flowers, food, and gifts to the house. I wrote thank-you cards to the strangers who had donated to the scholarship fund that had been set up for Laurel. I wrote over 800 cards in the course of a few weeks. I tried to read the books on grief and coping that people had sent me. I would quickly realize that reading about grief only made me more depressed. Nothing on television held my attention—the only thing I watched was the scrolling text on CNN with the audio turned off. I couldn't stand to listen to the non-stop media coverage of the attacks, the expert opinions, the eyewitnesses, the theories about how this unimaginable tragedy had happened. What I wanted was just the facts. I watched CNN for months, never fully understanding until much later why I had been compelled to do so.

I had found out about my husband's crash on CNN; this source of information was the only thing I felt I could trust.

4

IN MEMORY

"Home Free, eventually
At the ultimate healing we will be Home Free."

—Wayne Watson, "Home Free"

On September 21, 2001, the last day of summer, we held a memorial service for LeRoy at my church in Hamilton, Ontario. The Hamilton Mountain Seventh-day Adventist Church had been the setting for many family milestones: my parents' wedding in 1964, my dedication in 1966, and my baptism at age thirteen. LeRoy and I had been married in the church in 1998, and Laurel's dedication had taken place in December 2000. It seemed both appropriate and significant to have the service there. The last time a limousine had been parked in front of my family home was on my wedding day. How surreal it was to be getting into a limousine to attend a memorial service for LeRoy. I was lost in thought on the way there. When we pulled up in front of the church, a hand reached out to help me out of the car. It was my father's hand, the same hand that had helped me out of a limousine on my wedding day three years earlier.

Before I even entered the church, I could feel myself falling apart. My mother was carrying Laurel for me as we made our way in. I had finally seen my mother two days earlier when I arrived in Hamilton. I had come into the house and ran to her. We both cried for a long time. For the next couple of days, my mom cared for Laurel and helped me make the final arrangements for the service. As we entered the church, I remember telling my mom that I couldn't cry because if I did, I would never stop. As we made our way to the front pew, we were amazed at how many people had come to pay their respects. Family and friends—some I hadn't seen since high school—had found out about the service and came to mourn LeRoy, even though many had never met him. Representatives from both the city of Hamilton and the province of Ontario had called our pastor to ask permission to be in attendance, and with only a few days' notice, the city of Hamilton contacted our pastor to arrange for the Hamilton Police Guard to present both the Canadian flag and the

American flag in honor of LeRoy.

The service was my first glimpse into how deeply the world had been affected by the September 11 attacks. A letter from Jean Chrétien, the Prime Minister of Canada, was read at the service by Sheila Copps, the Member of Parliament for Hamilton, and presented to me. Other local political dignitaries were also in attendance. The church was packed. I saw people in the pews that I hadn't seen in ten, twenty years. There were high school teachers, friends of my parents; so many people who had never met LeRoy. I was overwhelmed by all the gestures of sympathy. I hadn't lived in Canada since 1989; LeRoy was an American citizen. But I was one of their own, and by extension, so was LeRoy.

A single candle stood at the front of the church next to a picture of LeRoy taken on our wedding day. I had selected the songs and the Scripture readings for the service, needing the reassurance of the promises of a life beyond this one, an eternal life with no suffering or pain, where I would be with LeRoy again. Although LeRoy had been raised Catholic, he had told me years earlier that if anything happened to him, he wanted his service to be in our church. LeRoy had started to question his faith when he was twelve years old, after the death of his father. He told me how he and his siblings had prayed together after their father had collapsed from a stroke. His father lived for a few more weeks, but never made it back home and passed away in the hospital.

Although he attended church sporadically while at the Air Force Academy, LeRoy's disillusionment with the Catholic Church grew and eventually he stopped going altogether. We had visited his dad's grave one day while out on Long Island. When I asked him where he believed his father was, he pointed to the ground. Unlike LeRoy, I did believe in eternal life, a life free from sickness, pain, and death. We had talked a lot about our spiritual beliefs before we married. It was important to me to raise our children in a home where we shared the same values. LeRoy started to attend church with me while we were dating, and in the six years we were together, I saw him slowly regain his faith. For the first time in his life, he was reading the Bible, sometimes asking me questions and discovering a truth that made sense to him.

During those first few days after LeRoy's flight went down, I questioned having a service at all. Why should I? How could it possibly help me? But eventually I understood how important it was to give LeRoy's friends and colleagues an opportunity to say their goodbyes. Since there were many people who could not attend the service in Canada, we held a second service a week later in New Jersey. Our home church couldn't accommodate more than a hundred people, so our pastor suggested the gymnasium of Meadow View Junior Academy, a Seventh-day Adventist elementary school in southern New Jersey.

My mom was not yet ready to get on a plane. Laurel and I had been driven to Canada by my friends Pam and Phil, who had driven to my home as soon as the U.S.-Canadian border had reopened and had been able to drive Laurel and I back to Canada for the service there. To get back to New Jersey, the only option we would consider was the train. It took over twelve hours to get back and it was exhausting, trying to hold my emotions together while caring for Laurel. My mom was a big help, but I could see she was having a difficult time as well. We had less than a week before the second memorial took place on Friday, September 28, 2001. There were over 800 people in attendance.

I had refused requests by the media to have cameras at the memorial service, but when we went outside for the twenty-one gun salute, the camera crews were all there, with their huge lenses pointed at us. Seven airmen shot their rifles three times, and Laurel started to cry. A female officer handed me a folded flag. "On behalf of the President of the United States, the Department of the Air Force, and a grateful nation, we offer this flag for the faithful and dedicated service of Major LeRoy W. Homer, Jr." If I didn't take the flag from her, then this couldn't be happening. But of course, I did take it. The part of me that would never embarrass or hurt LeRoy in any way was the part of me that accepted the flag.

Afterwards, I stood in a receiving line much like at a wedding. When LeRoy and I had been planning our own ceremony, we both were disappointed with our friends who had not made more of an effort to attend. Both LeRoy and I had been in several wedding parties over the years and had attended numerous out-of-town weddings, despite the additional travel expense. We felt that if a friend invites you to be with them on one of the most important days of their life, then you should make your best effort to be there. LeRoy even joked about it when we were receiving the RSVP cards for our wedding. There were two "choices"—wedding or funeral—and he preferred that his friends attend his wedding. He wouldn't know if they came to his funeral.

I couldn't help thinking about that conversation as I saw the faces of people who had not made it to our wedding. I stood in the receiving line for over an hour. Finally it was over. I could go home and get back to bed.

5

BRINGING LEROY HOME

"Mysteriously and in ways that are totally remote from natural experience, the gray drizzle of horror induced by depression takes on the quality of physical pain."

—William Styron

Most of my nursing career was spent caring for children with cancer. Sometimes one of my young patients would die after several years of care and suffering. I went through difficult times coping with these deaths, but I figured out ways to deal with the losses so I could continue to work in pediatric oncology, a specialty I had grown to love. Sometimes I stayed in touch with the family years after they had lost a child. Most of my patients survived, beat their cancer, and would sometimes return to visit, bigger and taller with full heads of hair. For my patients who were terminally ill, I knew if I did my job right they would die without pain and without fear. But knowing all of this, and witnessing death firsthand on a regular basis, did nothing to help me now.

LeRoy and I were both planners. We would talk and plan and dream, about when we thought we would move into another house, when we would have another baby, how we would adjust our lives if our parents needed to live with us one day. We talked about places in the world we wanted to see. LeRoy was already planning our tenth wedding anniversary; he wanted to go back to French Polynesia where we had spent our honeymoon. We even talked about LeRoy's retirement flight. I had never actually seen LeRoy at the controls, flying the airplane. After takeoff, only flight attendants were allowed in the cockpit. I wanted to see LeRoy actually doing this job he loved so much. He told me the wives usually flew on their husband's last flight before retirement, and would sit in the cockpit for part of the time. "Can you wait until I'm sixty to fly with me?" he asked once. "Definitely!" I had replied.

But now all the plans we had made were erased. I felt as if someone had taken a giant eraser and wiped away everything I had carefully set in place for my future, for my life. In the weeks afterwards, when I was too overwhelmed to make decisions, it was easiest to stick with our original plan. When faced with the decision of where I was going to live, I chose to stay in New Jersey. LeRoy and I had started to house hunt just that August in central New Jersey. We hoped to expand our family and also lessen LeRoy's commute to the New York airports. But we still wanted the proximity to both sides of our families, and wanted to live in an area with good schools for Laurel. So I stuck with the plan, except I no longer needed to find a home closer to the airports. Of course, I couldn't resolve every issue like this. The new reality I was living in had brought with it scenarios we could never have imagined. But I noticed that if I was patient, I would discover what it was I needed to do. This was the first time I could remember where I had no idea what path I was supposed to take. But I realized that not having my own plan allowed me to hear and understand the little voice inside of me, the voice that was guiding my decisions now.

The first time I went out by myself was October 1. I hadn't been able to attend the memorial services of the other three United pilots. I knew their names and a little bit about them through Steve and Marty. Ellen Saracini's husband, Victor, had been the captain of United 175. Miriam Horrocks's husband, Michael, had been first officer of that flight. Sandy Dahl was the wife of Jason Dahl, the captain of LeRoy's flight, United 93. I had looked up all of the men's names in LeRoy's log books. He kept a handwritten log book of everyone he had flown with and I found out he had flown with both Victor and Michael a couple of months earlier in August. Flight 93 would have been the first time LeRoy and Jason would have met.

I wanted to write to each of the women and I wanted to select the cards myself. All my family had gone home after the memorial service in New Jersey, leaving my mom behind to stay with me for awhile. Since the store was close to my home, I thought I would be able to do this quick errand without being recognized as the widow who had been on the front page of the local newspapers. I drove to a local card store about a mile from my house. I had a Post-it note on my dashboard reminding me where I was going and what I needed to purchase. My brain felt foggy and my mind would wander, so I constantly had to write notes to myself to help me stay focused. It felt weird to be out in public by myself. My sister Heather had been with me on the few occasions I had left the house, but she had returned home, and now I was on my own.

I felt exposed, and somewhat anxious, because sometimes people would recognize me. "Oh, you're the widow of that pilot," I had already heard on more than one occasion, most recently when I had run into a craft store to find a few frames to display LeRoy's photos at the memorials. But no one seemed to notice me as I made my way around the store that day. I took my cards up to the counter and handed the saleswoman some money.

As she handed me my change, she said, "Thank you. Have a nice day."

Have a nice day? I felt like I had been punched in the stomach. I could feel the tears coming. *Have a NICE day?* I wanted to scream. Instead I drove home and went back to bed.

* * *

I had been told early on by the FBI and the Somerset County coroner that there were very few human remains at the crash site, due to the velocity at which the plane hit the ground. Since the impact of the plane had caused a massive explosion that led to immediate incineration, everyone who had been on the plane had to be identified by DNA. I would later find out from Wally Miller, the Somerset County coroner, that they had only been able to recover approximately 2.6 percent of the remains of each person on the plane.

FBI agents came to my home to collect LeRoy's razor and toothbrush to obtain a DNA sample within the first week. I had been told they would be coming, so I was able to deal with this part of the process without too much difficulty. I knew I wanted LeRoy to be identified and this was what I had to do to have that happen. They gave me a form that had several notification options: I could be informed when LeRoy's remains were initially identified, and then every time more remains were recovered and identified; or, I could be notified just once when the identification process was complete. I chose the latter.

I got the call in late October, a few days after Laurel's birthday. There was still a part of me that wanted to believe LeRoy was out there somewhere, and that this heartache was all a big mistake. But when the phone call came from Wally to tell me they had identified LeRoy's remains, it felt like a fresh blow, like I was back at the beginning. Wally was professional but empathetic. He asked me if I had any questions. I asked what part of LeRoy's body had been recovered. Wally asked me if I really wanted to know. I could tell by the tone of his voice that I wouldn't want to know, so I declined. With this further confirmation that LeRoy was not coming home, I sat on the steps of my doorway and cried.

* * *

Laurel's first birthday was October 25. LeRoy and I had already decided we wouldn't have a big first birthday party. We wanted to be able to spend time with her without having to entertain a big group of people. We would have a big party when she was old enough to really enjoy it. This was one of those times when I was able to "stick with the plan."

At the time, my mom and my friend Dawn and her little girl Alix, who was five weeks younger than Laurel, were staying with me. My mom had come to the memorial in Bordentown, New Jersey in late September and would stay a month. Dawn came a few days before my mother left, to help with Laurel and be there for me, giving me a few extra days before I would be on my own. On Laurel's first birthday, we took the kids to a local kiddie gym for the morning. I dressed Laurel in the lavender top with leggings decorated with the moon and stars that her dad had bought her a couple months earlier while on a Boston layover. Laurel and Alix played in the plastic colored balls, crawled through tubes, and rode a miniature merry-go-round. Back home, we tried to get Laurel to open her presents but she wasn't very interested and kept crawling out of the room. I smiled and took pictures through the pain in my heart; LeRoy was not there to see how funny she was.

Digna had made dinner and brought it over for us. There we were—my mom, Dawn, and I—sitting around the kitchen table with Laurel and Alix in their highchairs. We all put on our happy faces for Laurel's sake. Her face lit up with the sweetest little smile when she saw the candle on her cake. And although she didn't eat too much, she did a pretty good job of spreading the frosting everywhere; we even found some in her ears. After pictures, my mom had to put her right into the tub, the bathwater turning blue from all the colored frosting. Laurel had a good birthday—the kind of birthday LeRoy and I had planned.

In November I attended the Flag Run. Organized by United and American Airlines, this was an event to symbolically complete the four flights that had crashed. The flag had started its journey in Boston on October 11 and would finish at the beach by LAX Airport on November 11. Three hundred and fifty volunteers had helped organize the 3872-mile cross-country journey. I, along with family and friends of the crews of the four flights, would be carrying the flag for the last mile of the run. I arrived at LAX on November 10—exactly six years to the day that I had driven there to meet a guy named LeRoy Homer for the first time. From the moment I entered the airport, I was filled with emotions as my mind flashed back to six years earlier. I struggled, trying to understand the journey that had brought me back here on this day of all days.

My friends who still lived in Southern California met me in Los Angeles to walk the last mile. It was good to be with friends who knew LeRoy from his trips back and forth to California when we had started dating. Ellen Saracini and Sandy Dahl were both there, too. Ellen's husband, Victor Saracini, had been the captain on United Airlines Flight 175, and Sandy's husband, Jason, had been with LeRoy on Flight 93.

I first met Ellen at LeRoy's memorial service in New Jersey. I hadn't expected her to attend, and was surprised when Steve approached me to say, "Ellen Saracini is here, and she would like to meet you."

"Who?" In the past three weeks, I had heard the names of the other pilots' families—Dahl, Saracini, and Horrocks—but at that moment I couldn't comprehend who he was referring to.

"Ellen Saracini. Her husband was the captain of 175."

When he said this, and I finally understood who he was talking about, I felt this desperate, frantic feeling, like I needed to get to Ellen right away. I jumped up from my seat and looked around to see if I could figure out who she was.

Steve led me towards her. As soon as we were close enough, we reached out and clung to each other. Through the tears I tried to speak, to tell her she was the only one in the room who knew what this felt like. That was the moment Ellen and I became friends and allies. I am still, to this day, amazed she had the strength to attend not only LeRoy's service, but the services of other crew members from both United and American Airlines. We have shared so much throughout the years, and she is still the person I look to when I struggle. She always gives me what I need, whether it's tough talk to get me going or a laugh with our own brand of "widow" humor. "I wish I'd never met you," Ellen and I said to each other in those first months.

I met Sandy Dahl for the first time at the Flag Run. All of the family members and friends who had flown out to complete the last mile of the walk had gathered in a local hotel lobby. That was when one of the pilots introduced me to Sandy. It felt a lot like when I had met Ellen, that the tragic way we had lost our husbands had bonded us in a manner unlike any other friendship. As we walked that last mile with the rest of the family members and friends of the people who had died on board the four flights, along with employees of both United and American airlines, Sandy and I had an opportunity to get to know each other by talking about LeRoy and Jason. We knew LeRoy and Jason had been a team in the truest sense of the word. These two men, who would have met for the first time in New Jersey's Newark Airport flight office, had fought together to try to keep control of their cockpit. Without even expressing this fully, Sandy and I became a team.

I would eventually meet Miriam in February 2002. I had heard she was really struggling emotionally, more so than the rest of us, so I was a little anxious. But like Ellen and Sandy, Miriam now shared something with me, an experience that made potentially awkward moments nonexistent.

It was at the Flag Run that I decided I wanted to complete LeRoy's flight. Even though the Flag Run had been a beautiful, symbolic way to complete the flights, it had ended in Los Angeles. LeRoy's flight had been headed to San Francisco.

Ellen had recently completed Victor's flight, flying from Boston to Los Angeles, the destination of United Airlines 175 before it crashed into the South Tower of the World Trade Center. Greg Downs, Victor's best friend and a United Airlines pilot, had been the one to fly Ellen and her girls to Los Angeles. It was such a beautiful tribute, and I wanted to do the same for LeRoy. So at the beginning of December, I started making plans to complete the flight. It seemed like something LeRoy would have wanted me to do. My parents would travel to New Jersey after the holidays to look after Laurel while I made the trip.

A few days before Christmas, Greg Downs, one of our Air Line Pilots Association (ALPA) representatives, called and said he had something he wanted to bring to me, something that had been recovered from the crash site. I had met Greg shortly after September 11. He had been extremely supportive in helping the pilots' families; any information he had concerning our situation, be it from United Airlines, the union, or any of the government agencies, he would call to share with us. Sometimes he would call just to check in and say hello.

I already knew that Greg was bringing me LeRoy's recovered dog tags, the ones he had kept on his keychain. So when Greg dropped off a small box, I knew they'd be inside. Greg stayed for a few minutes, but wanted me to be alone when I opened the box. He told me that he knew the contents could not bring LeRoy back, but he hoped it would help in some way. So when he left, I opened the box, expecting to find the dog tags. But there was something else. It was LeRoy's wedding band. I began to cry. I don't know how the recovery workers knew whose ring it was; neither of our names was engraved on the metal. The inscription inside was the Bible verse we had chosen for our wedding ceremony: "the greatest of these is love." In all my conversations with the FBI, no one had ever asked about a wedding band. The only explanation I could imagine was that it had been found on LeRoy's hand.

I was grateful to have the ring back. At the same time, here was further confirmation of a fact I refused to fully believe.

* * *

With Christmas approaching, I restarted my antidepressants on my doctor's advice. I had taken the
medication in the weeks after September 11 but had
stopped when I decided the medication would just
delay the inevitable pain. It would be better to just face
things upfront.

I had started back to work at the beginning of
November. It had been an easy transition because as
the holidays neared, the sales representatives I worked
with were not as busy, and therefore didn't require my
services as much as they did at other times of the year.
During a typical month, I would be booked for two to
three presentations a week in area hospitals; however,
it would take several months to book new dates. I had
gotten through Thanksgiving okay. My sister had
come to visit and the three of us had gone to a nice
restaurant for a quiet dinner. As a nurse, I should have
known better. But personally and professionally, I
hadn't had much experience with depression.

I soon realized that the medications didn't make
me happy at all, and my pain was still ever present.
What the medications did was help me function—to
help me out of bed in the morning and to improve my
concentration, which had been lacking for weeks. With
Christmas coming, I went through the motions as best
I could. I took Laurel to see Santa, and made plans to
go home to Canada to spend Christmas with my family.

The trip to Canada was uneventful. It was harder traveling with Laurel by myself and my emotional state was deteriorating as each day drew me closer to Christmas. In the past, we had split Christmases between the two families; we had usually been able to spend Christmas Eve with LeRoy's family, which was when they opened their gifts and had their holiday meal, and then we would fly to Canada early Christmas morning, the day my family celebrated. After Laurel was born, we decided it would be too hectic to try to do both, and that we would have to spend Christmas with each side of the family every other year.

The year Laurel was born, her first Christmas, we spent it in Canada. Most of our friends and family were meeting her for the first time. Now here we were, a year later, and everything was completely different. I had no interest in seeing anyone or celebrating. Even with the medication, Christmas was awful. LeRoy had loved Christmas, which made it that much more difficult to bear without him. Although my work schedule had been light, adjusting to a new routine of me getting up every morning with Laurel by myself, getting us dressed and out the door, and then picking her up at the end of the day, coming home and making dinner for her, while handling all the household chores by myself, had exhausted me. I was both emotionally and physically drained. I spent the majority of my holiday visit in bed, thankful that I had help with Laurel and could just be alone and retreat into myself.

My whole family had come together for Christmas. My sister had come in from Atlanta and my brother and his wife lived only a short distance away from my parent's home. On Christmas Day, my dad had suggested a moment of silence for LeRoy. After that, it was pretty much downhill for all of us. We opened presents. There weren't many because we had decided that since no one was up for shopping, we would just have small gifts. I'm not even sure if I got Laurel any presents that year. But fortunately she was still little enough to not know any different.

* * *

It was already March 2002 when I received the call. I had just walked in the door of the Philadelphia Convention Center with a friend to attend the Flower Show, thinking it would be a good distraction, and a chance to get out of the house. My phone rang. It was Steve, calling to tell me United had notified him that the FBI had released LeRoy's remains and they would be arriving at the Philadelphia Airport later that day. "Is it okay with you if I meet the flight?" he asked.

One of the first things LeRoy had done after we were married was to purchase *The Beneficiary Book*, a place where all our important information could be stored. There was a section labeled "Final Wishes." Here, he had written in the names of friends he wanted as pallbearers at his funeral. "The guys from my wedding party and Steve," he had written. Steve had been someone LeRoy respected; he had served his active duty career at McGuire and been hired at United before the other guys had completed their active duty. LeRoy had followed Steve's example and continued on in the U.S. Reserves after his active duty ended.

Steve, dressed in his United Airlines uniform, went to meet his friend's last flight home. I left the convention center, the possibility of a day's distraction gone, and made my way back to New Jersey. When I arrived home and checked my messages, there was a call from a nearby funeral home alerting me that a local news station had called the parlor in an effort to track me down. Somehow the media had found out about LeRoy's remains being flown home. I was horrified. Did they want a shot of the coffin? Of me crying? I didn't return the station's call. The funeral director came to my home to have me sign the necessary paperwork so I could avoid the cameras entirely.

6

UNITED AIRLINES

"From all of us here at United Airlines,
thank you for flying the friendly skies."

—LeRoy Homer, First Officer, United Airlines

One of the first times I visited LeRoy's childhood home where his mother still lived, he showed me his scrapbook. As a kid, he would cut out newspaper articles about airplanes, some even about airplane crashes. His bedroom was all about airplanes. There were airplane models he had built, and airplane posters lined the walls. Most of his aviation memorabilia featured United Airlines. He had always wanted to fly for United, even as a child. He considered them the best in the industry.

I began to develop my own impression of United Airlines after September 11. In those first few days, I talked to various company representatives, some by telephone, and others in person. During these conversations, there was always someone there to represent the Air Line Pilots Association (ALPA). It didn't take long for me to understand why I needed them.

United Airlines had assigned someone to stay with each of the pilot's families on September 11. Since Steve and Marty were already here, they were asked to stay and would take turns spending the day at my house. On September 13, Steve received a call from United's management. They wanted to wire me $25,000. I didn't understand why they were giving me money, and regardless, I didn't want it. Steve encouraged me to take it. Management had told him there were no strings attached and that I might need money for incidentals in the next few days. Family members and friends would be flying in from all around the world. This money could help with travel arrangements. I gave Steve my banking information so the funds could be deposited. Written verification of United's transfer of funds and the conditions under which I had accepted the funds were never provided. Several weeks later I would receive a letter from United Airlines' attorneys indicating the money had been "an advance against any future sum which would be realized by settlement or a judgment."

On September 14, Mr. Jim Goodwin, the CEO of United Airlines, called to offer his condolences.

Eighteen United employees had been killed. I couldn't understand why it had taken him three days to make the calls. Months later, during the time Ellen, Sandy, Miriam, and I were trying to get back the benefits we had lost, I read an article in *The Washington Post*, detailing how United Airlines' management had gone to Congress within a day of the crash to seek protection from impending lawsuits. The phone call was brief, lasting about a minute. He said he was calling on behalf of United and wanted to offer his condolences, and if there was anything I needed, I should let Steve or Marty know and they would notify the person or department, depending on what was needed. I realized he was under a lot of strain making these calls, but his call, coming when it did, felt stiff and almost perfunctory; I felt it lacked sincerity.

On September 18, United sent me a handwritten payroll statement indicating LeRoy's "final earnings." Why were they giving me this piece of paper? Where was the computer-generated statement we usually received? I gave the paper to Steve, and said, "I don't want this piece of paper. Where is his real statement?" Things were happening too fast, so fast it seemed that United hadn't taken the time to print out LeRoy's payroll statement. As it turns out, the statement wasn't correct. The ALPA pilot representatives, who had been coming by periodically to check on me and to make sure the company was doing what they were supposed to, were the ones who realized the error. United had calculated final earnings for LeRoy and the other pilots up to the time of the crash. Contractually, United was required to pay for the entire month of September. ALPA went to United about this and I received a second check in November 2001, with a letter that stated United had discovered an "adjustment needed to be made," and additional pay was due for the month of September. I have a feeling the "adjustment" never would have been discovered had it not been for ALPA.

A couple weeks later I received the benefits package, which outlined the assistance I would be receiving from United. A representative from the airline brought the package of information to my house and reviewed it with me. I had originally been told by United that they would be sending my benefit packet to me on September 14, 2001. However there were delays and I didn't receive the packet until several days after that. Steve, who had been with me that day, sat in while the United representative explained my benefits. I listened without hearing or processing the information. The paperwork we read through indicated we would no longer have dental and medical coverage for Laurel, and I would only be covered through the end of 2001. But I don't remember hearing that when we read through the packet. I did however read the document later on and became aware that I was going to lose my medical and dental coverage. The one piece of information that did pierce through my foggy consciousness was this: "Travel benefits for parents cease with the death of the employee. Please convey this information to LeRoy's mother Ilse Homer, if she survives him."

LeRoy's dependents—Ilse, Laurel, and I—received travel privileges, which meant we could fly on any United Airlines flight for a small service fee, as long as there was an empty seat. Now I needed to tell my mother-in-law, who had just lost her son, that she would no longer be able to travel on United in a seat that would ultimately go empty. In addition, companion passes for our friends and family members were "not extended to the surviving spouse or any eligible children." When my parents had flown to London with LeRoy and me, we had used these companion passes. Now if I used my travel benefits, I would have to travel alone.

I couldn't understand why United was taking away our benefits, benefits of little or no cost to them. LeRoy had died in service to this company. Even as United's management assured us they would do everything they could to assist us, in actuality it seemed they were trying to do as little as possible. United's human resources department, called "the People Division" at the time, kept referring to what they were able to do in relation to the contract. For example, when I questioned why Ilse would lose her travel privileges, I was told United was bound by their contract with the pilots. Yet, ALPA, the union, had drafted and passed two resolutions, first in October 2001 and then in July 2002, which stated, "Any benefits enjoyed by the families of United pilots who were killed in the performance of their duties [will] be paid for life, and be it further resolved that any benefits that UAL [United Air Lines] management has taken away from our deceased brothers' families be restored immediately and for life." ALPA wanted us to have our benefits, regardless of what the contract said.

Since nothing like this had happened before, there would be no way any contract could begin to address the uniqueness of this situation. Hadn't United Airlines had an obligation to keep LeRoy safe? How could this company treat its employee families with what I could only feel was indifference? The outpouring of support from across the nation and around the world stood in stark contrast to the seeming lack of sympathy from United Airlines. I could only imagine how LeRoy would feel, knowing that the company of which he had been so proud to be a part had shown little concern for what we were going through. I knew that LeRoy would have expected more. I wasn't going to let United let me down. At the minimum, Laurel and I deserved some respect for what LeRoy had been through.

Ellen, Sandy, and Miriam felt as strongly as I did. We requested a meeting through the ALPA representatives with United's interim CEO, Jack Creighton. Jim Goodwin, the man who had been United's CEO on September 11, had been ousted from his position in October 2001, after he made statements predicting that United Airlines would not survive given the attacks. Mr. Goodwin was given $5.7 million to buy out the remaining three years of his contract. His golden parachute also included over $2 million in cash, stock, and benefits. This was the man whose comments had caused the airline inestimable harm. The October 30, 2001 edition of the *New York Times* published an article by a reporter named Laurence Zuckerman in which losses since Mr. Goodwin's comments were estimated at $20 million a day. The irony of having to fight for our benefits while Mr. Goodwin received a huge severance was not lost on the four of us.

Mr. Creighton refused to meet with us until Miriam called United's headquarters and threatened to fly to Chicago, United's major hub, and chain herself to an airplane. The meeting with Mr. Creighton and the four wives was arranged, and took place in New York.

One of the first things we discussed when we met with Mr. Creighton and our ALPA representatives was our medical and dental benefits. At the time, most of us, including our children, were receiving mental health therapy. Our children also required routine checkups and medical care. We explained to him how insulting it was to receive a letter informing us that our husbands' parents could no longer travel at reduced rates. In actuality, my mother-in-law Ilse had used her travel benefits only once in the six years the benefits had been in effect, so it was more the principle of the matter than anything else.

In addition to the benefits, we also expressed our concerns with the way the airline had handled notification on September 11. Ellen, Sandy, Miriam, and I all had different stories of how we had learned about our husband's deaths, each one worse than the next. Sandy's mom had been visiting, and was with her when she received the call. Ellen was on the phone with the flight office when Greg, a United pilot and Victor Saracini's best friend, who had already found out about the crash of United 175 from Bob Spielman, the New York chief pilot, came charging through her door. Miriam, who was not at home at the time, received a message on her answering machine from the New York flight office, asking her to call them back. As the wife of a pilot, she knew this call was a red flag.

United ALPA representatives had been in touch with pilots from American Airlines who had knowledge of the pilots' families of Flights 11 and 77. American

Airlines had a notification system in place that was used on September 11. The wives of the American Airlines pilots killed on Flights 11 and 77 were notified in person. We wanted to offer our thoughts on improving the company's crisis response so that no one would ever have to experience what we went through. As one of the United pilots who had been directly involved with the families stated in a letter to the company detailing flight operations on what happened on and immediately after September 11, "A United plane will crash again. Maybe not under these circumstances, but regardless, things need to be handled much better than they were in [this] situation."

The four of us had come up with concrete suggestions on how United could improve their crisis plan to avoid employees receiving news of a crash over the phone. We asked to see the crisis plan that was in place on September 11. What we received was a general one-page document from the Emergency Response Manual titled *Domicile Chief Pilot* followed by eight bullet points. The only bullet point in the plan that mentioned the pilots read: "Protects pilots' interest and cares for the needs of pilots and family members." That was it. That one sentence was the plan United had in place for the pilots' families in the event of a crisis. The rest of the plan called for notification to World Headquarters (WHQ); assistance to the station manager if there was an accident at the airport; coordination with Flight Operations, People Service, and ALPA; obtaining flight crew statements; and then filing a report. This was the extent of the plan.

There were other travel benefit issues that we brought to Mr. Creighton's attention during this meeting. We had had our companion passes revoked, which meant we could no longer have a friend fly with us at the discounted rate. Twenty-four flight segments were awarded to every employee each year, to be given to whomever they chose. These were the passes my parents had used when they had accompanied LeRoy and me to London in August 2000. As it stood, we would no longer be receiving those. As Sandy pointed out during the meeting, she had already lost her husband. Now while she could still travel as an employee spouse, she would not have the ability to bring a friend along, even though as a widow, she would need one more than ever.

We asked to have our interline travel benefits restored. Interline travel allows one airline employee to fly on another airline at a reduced rate. These tickets could be purchased at the airport right before getting on a flight. LeRoy and I had used interline passes to travel on Air Canada when we visited my family.

We also wanted our husband's seniority to accrue for employee pass travel. If we couldn't accrue seniority, our ability to actually use the benefit would decrease over time, since empty seats are awarded based on this seniority.

The meeting with Mr. Creighton was highly emotional. We had lost our husbands and now four months later, fighting to keep our benefits seemed unfair. Mr. Creighton listened to all of our concerns. He promised he would see what he could do and get back to us as soon as possible. I felt somewhat positive after the meeting. We had been heard; now that Mr. Creighton understood the issues, United could start working towards resolving them.

We received a written response from Mr. Creighton about a month after our meeting. His letter ignored much of what we had discussed with him. In regards to our medical benefits, he agreed to allow our families to continue to be covered. We would receive monthly invoices since we would be responsible for paying the monthly premiums which had previously been deducted from LeRoy's paychecks. As for our dental coverage, Mr. Creighton stated he "regrettably was not able to make any policy changes." And although he agreed "the form of notification was insensitive," he was not willing to provide travel benefits to the parents, as "it would be considered income to the person traveling and would need to be reported to the IRS." His letter made no mention of our concerns about the crisis response.

What we later found out when we received the 2002 UAL Corporation stockholders and proxy statement—and what Mr. Creighton had failed to acknowledge in regards to travel privileges—was that United board members are not only allowed to travel first class in available seats, but also in confirmed seats, with the airline reimbursing the income tax liability. The airline's own guidelines stated that directors, along with their spouses and dependent children, needed to "understand the business and have exposure to operations and employees." One director had travel "exposure" valued at $76,000, if he had actually paid for it. In addition, a director on United's board would receive free travel and cargo benefits for life after five years of service.

LeRoy had been an exemplary employee. The chief pilot had given me letters and accolades from his employee file in the first few weeks after September 11. Some were written by nervous fliers he had reassured or parents whose children had visited the cockpit. LeRoy—who was responsible for the lives of hundreds of people on any given flight, who grew up only wanting to work for this airline, who went to work on the worst day of his life, and died as a result—was not as important to United Airlines as its board members. And to top it off, the letter from Mr. Creighton incorrectly listed the four pilots' names. The letter read "our heroes LeRoy, Homer, Victor, and Michael." Captain Jason Dahl's name was included when we brought it to the attention of our ALPA friends. The letter was resent on March 26, 2002 with the names corrected and a note from Mr. Creighton's assistant, apologizing for the error.

I had decided early on that I would not sue the airline for the crash. When I had met with an estate attorney, to draw up a new will after LeRoy died, I was introduced to a personal injury attorney at the same firm. It had been explained to me that if I sued United, their insurance company would settle the claim, so I wouldn't be hurting the company, this company that LeRoy had spent his whole life wanting to work for.

Although United Airlines had failed to keep LeRoy safe, the people, the systems, and the agencies responsible for the safety of all Americans—including the Bush administration, the Immigration and Naturalization Service, the Federal Aviation Administration, the Federal Bureau of Investigations, and the Central Intelligence Agency—had all failed, too. I didn't think that suing United Airlines would make air travel safer. And since I believed that LeRoy had a crucial role to play in Flight 93 not reaching its intended target, suing didn't make sense.

Miriam had said it best. All four pilots—LeRoy,

Jason, Victor, and Michael—had been loving husbands and fathers, good men, great pilots, with two feet planted in the here and now, not in the future. They were content. We marveled at how uncanny it was, how similar they all seemed in the way they had embraced where they were in their lives. And then Miriam said, "They were chosen." She was right. I felt certain LeRoy wouldn't have wanted me to sue. But I felt just as certain he wouldn't have wanted me to allow United's attempt at not accepting any responsibility for family members of the eighteen employees who had died.

The four of us—Ellen, Sandy, Miriam, and I—were not about to let them off the hook for medical and dental benefits that cost them next to nothing, yet were imperative to our families. It was calculated that the cost to restore these benefits would be approximately $70,000 a year for all eighteen United employee family members who had died on September 11. And since the parental travel privileges were only available if there was an available seat, taking this benefit away seemed completely heartless. But even after ALPA had gone to the management on our behalf, we were left with Mr. Creighton's decision.

We figured if United's management wouldn't listen to us, maybe they would listen to the public, who regarded our husbands as heroes. I had done an interview with *Good Morning America* in the week after the attacks, and the producers had told me that if I ever needed a voice, I should let them know. Ellen, Miriam, and I appeared together on GMA in August 2002. Sandy was unable to make it because of a family emergency. We were there to represent the voices of all employees who had died on United Flights 175 and 93. The initial interview got exactly the reaction we had hoped for. United issued a statement defending themselves, which was read on air during our GMA interview:

United Airlines Statement

"It goes without saying that the events of Sept. 11, 2001 were catastrophic and devastating to the entire country, but the tragedy was especially felt at United Airlines. United lost 18 of its treasured employees, members of its family, in a way that personally struck at all of the United employees. Upon learning of that loss, United reacted with great sensitivity and emotion, and it reached out to the families of the lost employees in extraordinary ways. Indeed, the mandate to which we responded was to do as much for the families of the employees as could be legitimately done.

United remains extremely proud of the way it and its employees responded to this tragedy, even as it continues to share the grief of the families who lost their loved ones. United will never forget the families of those employees who lost their lives on Sept. 11."

Ellen, Miriam, Sandy, and I responded to United's statement by issuing our own press release:

United Wives Respond to Statement by United Airlines

"The recent statement of United Airlines, once again, indicates that United management fails to realize the nature of our grievances following the murders of our husbands on September 11, 2001. Our grievances are rooted in the lack of sensitivity in the days, weeks and months following the tragedy. Once again, they have taken refuge in what they consider the safety of the Union contract. Specifically, they have stated they have done as much as could be legitimately by contract. However, since no United employee has ever been murdered in the line of duty, the contract could not have begun to address the issues that would arise in a situation such as this.

While the Air Line Pilots Association and employees at United have been very supportive, compassionate and helpful during the last year, the senior management of United showed very little sensitivity to the loss of their eighteen employees on that fateful day. They have treated the deaths of these employees like accidents and certainly not the tragedy that it was in the eyes of everyone from children across America to Heads of State. The management at United Airlines, who had a responsibility to their employees, seem to have very little concern for the families, as they refuse to resolve the issues that have been presented to them.

During this same time period, United executives were spending countless hours and millions of dollars a day asking for a public bailout while also giving our former CEO a multi-million dollar buyout of his contract.

The management at United Airlines has stated they reached out to families in "extraordinary ways," yet make no mention of how this was done. Our husbands were loyal employees of United Airlines. We have not been treated with the respect deserving [sic] of our families, and no other

United employee or their family should
be treated in this manner. There need
to be changes made within the Board of
Directors and the senior management
at United Airlines, individuals not only
capable of restoring United Airlines'
profitability, but [who] will also respect
and value their employees, at this
employee-owned company."

Journalists were interviewing United employees
and passengers alike and people seemed shocked and
outraged at our situation. The reaction of the public
generated enough attention to help us get another
meeting with airline management. We met with Glenn
Tilton, United's new and present CEO, in October 2002,
just weeks after appearing on GMA.

Finally, in November 2002, over fourteen months
after losing our husbands, each of the wives received a
letter from United Airlines. My letter said in part, "You
made it clear we should look at LeRoy and all the other
members of the United family and make sure we do all
that is possible to respect these true heroes. As a result
of your efforts, and in LeRoy's name, you have made a
difference for United employees."

Dental benefits were restored. We would be required
to pay the monthly premiums, but would remain under
their plan for life. Space-available parental travel and
companion passes were also reinstated to all the
employees' families. Although we had never asked for

this, United promised in the letter that one of the future new plane purchases from Boeing, the B777, would be named "The Spirit of United" in honor of all United Airlines employees and customers on Flights 175 and 93; the letter also stated that we would be invited for the dedication. I have no idea if there is a B777 named "The Spirit of United," but none of the four wives were ever invited to any such dedication.

The letter also stated that United would work on getting our interline travel benefits reinstated, but we never received this benefit. When the four of us had initially set up our meetings with United, one of our most pressing concerns was that the airline needed a better crisis plan. Despite assurances from United about valuing our input, they never followed up.

In addition, United informed us of a special profile that would be built into their computer system, which "would alert all agents and flight crew of the significance of whom they are interacting with, so that they can ensure that these families are treated with the utmost sensitivity and respect." This special profile was never built. Instead we remained in the computer under our husbands' identification numbers. I have spent years dealing with the "glitches" in their computer system, which often doesn't recognize me as the surviving spouse of a United employee. I carry a special card, which was given to me by the airline to verify my status as a widow of an employee shortly after September 11, but the card doesn't help when customer service can't find me in the computer.

Each time I had a problem using spouse travel, I would try to call Bob Spielman, the chief pilot. They would eventually be able to locate me in the computer, but it was stressful traveling under these circumstances. Sometimes United's customer service agents were empathetic and made calls to supervisors to try to figure out why they couldn't find me in the system; other times they were rude and abrupt, seemingly not understanding how our travel benefits worked or believing that we even had travel privileges in the first place.

During one particularly bad experience, I had been traveling with Laurel—a toddler at the time—and my parents to an event honoring LeRoy. As I waited at the check-in counter at Chicago's O'Hare Airport for the system to recognize my status, I called the chief pilot on my cell phone. He spoke to the customer service representative and explained my situation. But by the time they found my information in the computer, the plane had taken off. We had to spend the night in an airport hotel.

Over the years, I would become so emotional when dealing with the customer service representatives that I decided to stop flying with United Airlines altogether.

If an airline employee was going to be grumpy or rude, at least it would not be the airline for which my husband died working.

7

THE STORYTELLERS

"Fame is a vapor, popularity an accident, and riches take wings. Only one thing endures and that is character."

—Horace Greeley

"Bombs are dropping in Afghanistan. Would Melodie like to comment?"

Back in October 2001 while my mom had been staying with me, she had answered the phone, because I was trying to avoid the calls from the media. I shook my head, and she told them, "No thank you, no comment."

At the time of the crash, I had no idea that my phone would ring for the next few years anytime anything happened related to September 11, Flight 93, terrorist attacks in other countries, or airport security. Sometimes I would look at my caller ID, and if the call log showed numbers from my local news affiliates, I would turn on my TV to see what was going on that necessitated my comment. Usually I didn't provide a statement. Sometimes it was because I wasn't in the right frame of mind; sometimes I honestly didn't have an opinion. Mostly I was just tired of these intrusions into my life.

As fiercely as I tried to protect my privacy, it would be invaded time and time again in ways I could never have imagined. For several years LeRoy and I had included a letter with our Christmas cards, sharing the news of our lives from the past year. The letter we sent out for Christmas 2000 was particularly special. Laurel had been born two months prior and we shared with our friends the thrill of new parenthood. For reasons I cannot understand, a guy who had been high school classmates with LeRoy decided to take our letter to the media, and excerpts from it appeared in a New York newspaper. This individual made himself out to be someone he was not—a close friend. We had no contact with him except for the annual Christmas card. I don't recall him coming to LeRoy's memorial, and I've never heard from him since. But he did manage to get his name in the paper.

The next invasion of privacy came courtesy of the *Philadelphia Inquirer*. The newspaper had contacted me in late September 2001. They were planning a tribute to local victims of September 11 in the weekend edition, and wanted me to verify some biographical information about LeRoy and provide a photo. At that point, I allowed the local newspapers to interview me; the *Philadelphia Inquirer* was the largest, located just a few miles from where I lived in South Jersey. I provided their editor with the verification and photo requested. When I went to the local 7-Eleven to pick up a copy of this tribute edition—I had been saving newspapers since the beginning of the ordeal, thinking one day Laurel would want them—I felt like someone had knocked the wind out of me. On the front page was a picture of LeRoy and Laurel, a personal photo, which I had never shared with anyone.

When I contacted the newspaper, I was told that a photographer had taken a picture of the collage of family photos we had displayed at our New Jersey memorial service. The newspaper's photographer claimed he had obtained permission to do this, but he "couldn't recall" the name of the family member who had granted him authorization. In their conversations with me, the newspaper had never indicated they had a photo they were planning to print in place of the one I had provided. The *Inquirer* apologized and agreed to purge the photo from their archives; however, the damage was already done. The photo had already been released to the public. Despite the newspaper removing it from their files, other individuals had gotten hold of the photo online, and posted it on various sites. Although the photo was always accompanied by LeRoy's biography, this was a personal photo that now anyone who looked for images of "LeRoy Homer" online could see. It was an intimate photo of my husband and my daughter, one never meant to be seen by strangers.

Truly, my anguish seemed to mean little to the media in their pursuit of a story. Such was my experience with *Dateline NBC*. In late September 2001, a producer called to interview me for a special on Flight 93 they were putting together called "No Greater Love." This was one of the first interviews I had done, and we spoke on the phone at length. I was asked very specific questions about my last hours with my husband, as well as details surrounding the day of the crash. It was excruciatingly painful to talk about it, and I felt like I was reliving the events all over again.

The special aired on October 2, 2001. *Dateline NBC* and its producers chose to use nothing from my interview. The only mention of the flight crew was that "they had probably been killed." They had wasted my time, and caused me additional pain by forcing me to talk about the events I had tried hard to suppress. I couldn't understand why this producer had wasted the time interviewing me, only to not use any of the information we'd discussed. When the same producer called me a year later, asking for permission to use a picture of Laurel for a follow-up to "No Greater Love," I reminded them of what had been done to my interview the year earlier and explained why I would not be participating. This was the first time I had spoken to the producer since the previous year. There wasn't much of a reaction or an apology. For this person, it seemed to be just business.

When someone would call to ask for an interview, there were times when an expression of condolence was heartfelt, but most of the time the "sorry for your loss" was perfunctory and unconvincing. I had decided early on that there would need to be a compelling reason for me to agree to any type of media interview or appearance. The process was long and tedious, and afterwards I felt emotionally drained. It wasn't until I decided to start a foundation in LeRoy's memory that I realized I could use the media to help get the foundation's message out.

The LeRoy W. Homer, Jr. Foundation was created by family and friends in May 2002. Its mission is to encourage and support young adults who want to pursue careers as professional pilots. The scholarship funds the first step on their career path—private pilot certification.

I had hoped that when I did interviews about the foundation, it would also give me an opportunity to correct some of the many different versions of "What Really Happened on Flight 93" that had spread since September 11. In most of the newspaper and magazine articles I had come across, the pilots were all but ignored. "They would have been killed immediately." But there was a lot that hadn't been reported. I had sent a message to LeRoy that morning when I had first called the flight office which read that I just wanted to make sure he was okay. About thirty minutes later, the cockpit received the message from the United dispatcher to be aware of cockpit intrusions because two aircraft had already hit the World Trade Center. These were the things I wanted the media to understand, to include in their news reports, especially since at the time, the media had not given much attention to any of the crew members in their stories. They didn't know about LeRoy's military background; they didn't know that LeRoy had been trained for hostile situations, or that he was still in the U.S. Air Force Reserves on September 11.

LeRoy had been the only pilot on the four flights who had prior knowledge of the morning's attacks and had alerted Air Traffic Control to the hijacking with his "May Day" call. The 9/11 Commission Report confirms struggling and fighting in a second transmission thirty-five seconds after LeRoy's initial "May Day" alert.

Despite sharing this information with the

journalists who interviewed me, the phone calls made from the plane were what seemed to grip people's attention. There had been several phone calls made from various individuals on the flight by both passengers and flight attendants. Some calls were made with GTE airphones, while others were using their cell phones. Although the information coming from various family members was quite contradictory, one thing seemed certain: the passengers and crew knew what had happened at the WTC and were planning to overtake the hijackers, in an attempt to thwart the attack and save their lives. What little I knew at the time about the events of that morning could not compete with a story that through the phone calls and a fair amount of speculation had given people something to cling to during a period of time when the United States needed inspiration more than ever. So, although I was being asked to do interviews, I didn't feel like I was heard when I talked about LeRoy and what I knew of the morning's events.

One of the unfortunate results of doing the interviews was the mail I began to receive. Letters addressed to me via the foundation's P.O. Box number started to arrive, all from men, most of whom were incarcerated. The envelopes bore return addresses from various state correctional facilities and were stamped with the words: "This is a prison." It didn't take me long to realize that the individuals sending these letters were more interested in me than in the foundation. It was a constant balance of deciding whether or not to do media interviews because although I needed the media attention for the foundation, I didn't like the attention I was receiving myself.

I spent a great deal of time educating the journalists who interviewed me about the differences between a pilot and a co-pilot. An interviewer would ask, "Was LeRoy the captain on the flight who actually flew the plane or was he just the co-pilot?" I'm not sure what these journalists thought the co-pilot did or if the misconception is perpetuated in movies and television, but I explained that both pilots, the captain and the first officer (or co-pilot), flew the airplane. Most trips were two legs, a trip to a destination and then the trip back. Each pilot flew one leg of the trip. The captain decided who flew which leg, and although the captain usually took the first round, sometimes he opted for the second leg. When one pilot was flying the airplane, the other pilot would make the radio calls to air traffic control along with any announcements to the passengers. Becoming captain was based on seniority and date of hire. If LeRoy had wanted to, he had enough seniority to become captain on a smaller aircraft such as the 737. But a 737 aircraft does not have the range to fly the long distances that LeRoy preferred, and the pay was better on the bigger airplanes, too.

The other question that I was asked on more than one occasion was: "Did you and LeRoy discuss the possibility of anything like this ever happening?" My response was that I doubted anyone who worked in the Twin Towers discussed with their spouse the possibility of a jumbo jet crashing into the building where they went to work every day. LeRoy and I didn't discuss it because no one would have imagined anything like this would ever happen.

There may be an assumption that when you are married to a pilot you worry about the plane crashing or being hijacked; maybe some men or women did. But I wasn't one of them. And neither were the other wives. In fact, Ellen is a certified pilot. Sandy was a United flight attendant at the time. We had all been asked this question, and felt equally perplexed by it. After all, I had helped LeRoy study for his annual check rides, which were emergency scenarios that took place in a simulator in Denver, Colorado, at the United Training Center. LeRoy was tested on what to do if an engine went out, if there was a fire on the plane, if the landing gear would not come down for landing, and various other scenarios. He had flashcards and I would help him prep. I had complete confidence that if an emergency presented itself he would handle the situation successfully.

I was first approached to be interviewed for a book about Flight 93 in 2002. Via an e-mail message to all of the Flight 93 family members, the author, Jere Longman, contacted us, requesting interviews for the book. I had no interest. It had only been a few months, yet I was already extremely wary of the media. Why would someone want to write a book, and about what? I had found the process of being interviewed to be quite difficult. Every time I was asked about September 11, I would be thrown back into the nightmare of that day. I didn't return his message. When my in-laws told me that they had been interviewed, I realized a decision to include LeRoy in this book had already been made. I decided I would listen to what the writer of the book had to say.

During our conversation, Mr. Longman explained that he wanted to honor the forty heroes, the thirty-three passengers and seven crew members on board Flight 93, by ensuring each of their stories was told. He was conflicted about the idea of making money off our tragedy and had decided he would make donations to foundations that had been set up in memory of individuals who had lost their lives on Flight 93. He didn't specify an amount and I didn't ask. Even after this conversation, I too was conflicted. I didn't want to participate in the book. But since LeRoy's family had already been interviewed, I decided I would go ahead, if only to guarantee that the published information about LeRoy was accurate.

I spoke to Mr. Longman several times in 2002. When I spoke to him a day or so after I had listened to the cockpit voice recorder (CVR), he asked me to discuss the recording. I explained to him that I had signed a confidentiality agreement with the Department of Justice and was not at liberty to tell him what I had heard. From the specificity of portions of text in *Among the Heroes,* some family members who had listened to the CVR had talked to Mr. Longman despite having signed confidentiality agreements.

The autobiographical information LeRoy's family had provided and my account of the day were included in Mr. Longman's book, which was published in 2002. The book was only the beginning. The first television movie *The Flight That Fought Back* came out in 2005 based on Longman's publication. Although I didn't watch the movie, I heard about it from people who had. Generally, people thought I had been involved in some way in the story portrayal, and seemed genuinely surprised when I told them I hadn't. I had received a letter from the Discovery Channel, as had the other family members, telling me about the project, but that was the extent of it. It didn't seem right to have parts of my life, a portrayal of what my morning might have been like, depicted on television, especially without my permission.

Then in 2006, another television docudrama, *Flight 93*, aired on A&E. Although I didn't watch this one either, inevitably I would get questions from people who had, questioning its accuracy. The second docudrama aired on a Sunday night; I remember because when I went to run my errands on Monday, the local store owners wanted to talk to me about it.

Being the only one in my small town who had lost someone on September 11 made me a bit of a target and an expected source of information. The community was surprised that I had never been contacted for permission to use my name, my likeness, or even to corroborate their portrayal of my family and me on that day. For example, in one of the movies, I have been told I am portrayed in a scene with my family all around me the day LeRoy's plane crashed. This hadn't happened because the border crossing between the United States and Canada had been closed and my mom had been on her cruise.

From what I have been able to gather, all these movies did was sensationalize the stories of the cell phone calls of the passengers to their family members, detailing their plan to retake the plane. Other cell phone calls had been made and not everyone had come forward with their stories, so the movies were a possible rendering into moments that we can never imagine or account for. I have still not seen these movies that have been described by friends who have seen them, as having a Hollywood ending with "the heroes" who saved the day.

Though I experienced the negative side of the media in many ways, I have also worked with journalists who I greatly admire, and who have been helpful over the years, in both personal and professional matters. In the first days after September 11, a local resident started a college fund for Laurel's education. The media was helpful in getting the information out as was evidenced by the large amount of donations which continued to pour in throughout the months that followed.

I appreciated the help I received when I established the foundation and needed the media's help to get the word out. And when the United Airlines' pilots' wives needed a forum to discuss how we were being treated by our husbands' company, *Good Morning America* gave us the opportunity to do so on their show. The one single aspect of the media that I disliked most, however, was the identity I was given as "the Flight 93 widow," "the pilot's widow," or "the 9/11 widow." Ellen, Sandy, Miriam, and I preferred to call ourselves "the wives." We still do. We refuse to be defined by that one single day, the single worst day of our lives.

8

THE COCKPIT VOICE RECORDER

"True heroism is remarkably sober, very undramatic.
It is not the urge to surpass all others at whatever cost, but the urge
to serve others at whatever cost."

—Arthur Ashe

Initially, most of the media coverage surrounded the World Trade Center. But then information about cell phone calls made by the passengers and crew on Flight 93 came to light. Most of the attention was focused on the calls made by four male passengers—Todd Beamer, Tom Burnett, Jeremy Glick, and Mark Bingham—who, after speaking with their loved ones and learning two planes had hit the World Trade Center, had informed their loved ones that they were planning to attempt to retake the plane from the hijackers. The prevailing theory at the time was that the pilots on all four flights were overtaken by the hijackers and immediately killed.

But there were discrepancies, some of which were noticed right away, and others that would be discovered later, during the September 11 commission hearings. For instance, several passenger phone calls had reported three hijackers were on board, but it was determined fairly quickly after the crash that there had been four hijackers.

Todd Beamer had called to report the hijacking. During the call, the phone operator said she overheard a flight attendant saying the men on the floor of first class were the captain and first officer; however, other callers identified one of the bodies as being a first-class passenger. One of the callers thought one of the hijackers might have had a gun; however, there was no evidence of a gun being used, and no firearms were discovered at the crash site. After the Moussaoui trial, the government offered information that Tom Burnett had not made four cell phone calls to his wife, as had been previously reported and published in *Among the Heroes*; he had used the GTE Airfone and had only been able to complete three phone calls. The phone calls made by the flight attendants, in which they described their situation and their plan to fight back against the hijackers, were given very little attention in the media reports. As the story of the phone calls gained momentum, the story of Flight 93 became almost entirely about the passengers, with little mention of the crew. On more than one occasion, various news outlets had reported that forty passengers were on board, instead of accurately reporting seven crew members and thirty-three passengers. Almost ten years later, an article published for the *Meadville Tribune* on February 17, 2011 reported that the Flight 93 memorial being built would honor the "40 passengers."

Right after the attacks, President Bush had defended his administration, insisting they had not had information specific enough to have prevented the September 11 terrorist attacks. But there were many unanswered questions. Why were relatives of bin Laden and his associates allowed to leave the United States eight days after the attacks, as reported in the *Washington Post*? Very few answers were provided by the government. My distrust for President Bush would increase as the months went by.

Within a few days of September 11, the FBI came to my house. One of the things they had previously discussed with me and Steve and Marty was the recovery of Flight 93's cockpit voice recording. To prepare for hearing the tape, they asked us to identify someone to listen who was a pilot, and would have a better idea of what was occurring and who also knew LeRoy and would be able to identify his voice. However, once it was determined that the majority of the thirty-minute recording captured only the conversations of the hijackers and not of LeRoy and Captain Dahl, the FBI no longer needed someone to identify LeRoy's voice. I was disappointed because the information I had heard on television, which focused on the cell phone calls made by some of the passengers, did not add up. Statements made by one passenger would contradict another. I had hoped knowing what was on the CVR would help me understand what had really happened.

I wanted to hear the CVR myself. I was afraid to hear it, but there had already been leaks to the media involving information on the recording, even as the Department of Justice assured family members that the CVR was in a secure location. I had already been blindsided by information, some accurate (I had found out there was a transcript of the CVR), most not (there had been conflicting information about the bodies that were seen, presumably dead, on the floor of the first-class cabin). Each time I would hear or read about the CVR, I would call Dave Novak at the Justice Department and he would verify if it was true or not. Knowing the recording and a transcript were out there, yet not knowing what was on it, was terrifying.

I had already been in a similar situation when I had unexpectedly received a phone call from a producer at ABC on November 15, 2001, only a few hours before that evening's *Primetime Live* would play the air traffic

control recordings of Flight 93. Friends came over to sit
with me as I heard LeRoy's voice yelling, "Get out of
here" and "May Day," as he alerted air traffic control to
the hijacking. Words cannot explain how painful it was
to hear this on a national broadcast. I didn't want this
to happen again with the cockpit voice recording, so I
wrote a letter to Robert Mueller, the director of the FBI,
in which I explained my reasons for wanting to hear
the CVR—or preferably, read the CVR transcript—in a
private setting. I received a response denying my
request; Mueller suggested "[I would not find] comfort
in the recording." So I wrote another letter.

March 4, 2002

Robert Mueller, Director
Federal Bureau of Investigation
J. Edgar Hoover Building
935 Pennsylvania Avenue, NW
Washington, DC 20535

Attn: Nancy Bronstein
Unit Chief
Office of Public and Congressional Affairs

Ms. Bronstein:

I received your response to my
letter dated January 17, 2002, [that
was] faxed to your office February 15,
2002. Your letter states that the FBI
did not release transcripts for the

<u>Newsweek</u> article. However, someone in the media saw those transcripts. Since sending my letter to your office, I have become aware of another journalist who has had contact and access to the transcript of the cockpit voice recorder. It appears that as long as someone has the right connections, they can obtain access to this "secure" information.

Within days of September 11, FBI agents contacted two of my husband's friends, who are also pilots with United Airlines. They were asked to go to Washington, D.C. to help identify my husband's voice on the cockpit voice recorder. I was informed at that time that I could not let anyone know this would be occurring. I told no one. The FBI was obviously not concerned with my having information at that time, if it were helpful to them. I surmise that when the FBI decided to not make use of my husband's friends, it now becomes apparent to you and your agency that you do not believe "victims' families would find comfort in the recording."

No one has any idea what a victim's family would find comforting, and unless your husband left for work on September 11, 2001, never to return, leaving you with a ten-month-old baby, you have no idea how I feel. When you receive 2.6 percent of your husband's remains six months after the last time you saw him, then maybe you can decide what is or is not comforting. Until then, it is very arrogant of you or your agency to presume anything.

My husband, as the co-pilot of Flight 93, has been hailed a hero. I have heard from many different government officials and agencies, including the FBI, that if there is anything they can do, I need only ask. My husband lost his life fighting for his aircraft, the safety of those on board the airplane, as well as those on the ground. However, that apparently is not enough for the FBI to want to help me in any way.

I am not a victim. I am a pilot's widow. I always knew that if my husband were to die in an airplane crash, that I would have access to the cockpit voice recorder or the transcript. I do not want to hear the recording. I do want to see the transcript. If your agency will not cooperate with my request, I will pursue this through other means, be it through the courts or through the media.

Sincerely,
Melodie Homer

Within a couple of weeks, I received a phone call from my local FBI agent, followed by an e-mail from Dave Novak from the Department of Justice, confirming that the family members of the Flight 93 crew and passengers would be allowed to hear the recording.

A Princeton hotel was chosen by the Department of Justice as the location where on April 18, 2002, the Flight 93 family members would finally be allowed to hear the recording. We were not permitted to take any notes, and we couldn't even bring paper of any kind into the room that had been designated for the listening sessions. The family members of the crew would hear the recording in the morning; the passengers' family members would have a separate session in the afternoon. Mental health counselors were on site in the event anyone needed assistance. The number of family members who were permitted to attend the listening sessions was limited, and we were all asked to sign confidentiality agreements.

The confidentiality agreements were necessary because the United States government was preparing their case against Zacarias Moussaoui, the individual who at the time was thought to have been the fifth hijacker on Flight 93. On December 11, 2001, Moussaoui had been indicted by a federal grand jury on six felony charges: conspiracy to commit acts of terrorism transcending national boundaries, conspiracy to commit aircraft piracy, conspiracy to destroy aircraft, conspiracy to use weapons of mass destruction, conspiracy to murder United States employees, and conspiracy to destroy property. The recording was to be used as evidence in the trial. Dave Novak, the Assistant District Attorney, was the person who explained this to us, stressing the importance of maintaining the confidentiality until the conclusion of the trial. He also indicated that if confidentiality was maintained, the Department of Justice would be more willing to provide additional information if it became available. The concern was that if information from the recording was made public prior to the trial, this could potentially compromise the U.S. government's case.

Finally, seven months after the crash, it was time to hear the CVR. Sandy and I sat together while we listened to the recording and read the transcript, which was simultaneously displayed on a screen at the front of the room. They played it through twice. The first time through I read the transcript and Sandy listened. After the recording looped for the first time, Sandy told me she thought I should listen. So after a short break to collect our emotions, the recording was played a second time, and this time I listened. As difficult as it was to hear, I knew I had made the right decision. The one question I had agonized over was immediately answered. LeRoy had not been killed by the hijackers.

The "experts" interviewed on various television newscasts, who surmised that the pilots would likely have been caught off guard and had their throats slit, were wrong. What these experts didn't know at the time was that LeRoy would have known immediately that something wasn't right. The United Airlines dispatcher had sent a message to the cockpit at 9:24 a.m. warning Jason and LeRoy: "Beware any cockpit intrusion. Two a/c [aircraft] hit World Trade Center." At 9:26, Jason Dahl responded: "Ed, confirm latest mssg plz—Jason."

LeRoy was an Air Force Academy graduate who had spent seven years in active military service; he was still serving in the Reserves as of September 11. He had been trained for quick thinking in hostile situations. He proved this when he made sure his radio microphone was open and shouted "May Day" to alert air traffic control at Cleveland Center of the hijacking. Cleveland Air Route Traffic Control is one of the most transitioned air traffic control centers in the country, and oversees the airspace over portions of Maryland, Michigan, New York, Ohio, Pennsylvania, and West Virginia.

There were sounds of papers being shuffled around as the two hijackers tried to control the aircraft. Although the autopilot was on, the hijackers attempted to manually fly the plane, causing the autopilot alarms to be heard throughout the recording. And then in the translated transcript, one of the hijackers said to the other in Arabic, "Inform them, and tell them to talk to the pilot. Bring the pilot back." There were two voices heard on the CVR. I can only assume the "them" they were referring to were the other two hijackers. The pilot they were referring to was LeRoy. Evidence found within days of the crash did not place LeRoy in the cockpit when the plane went down. There hadn't been any explanation given for this, and I hadn't thought much about it. After listening to the recording, Sandy identified Jason's voice as the male heard in the cockpit at the beginning of the recording. Jason's remains had been found in the cockpit. What he is saying is unclear on the CVR, although he is repeatedly told to "stop" and "lie down." Then the sounds go silent.

I will never know why LeRoy was not immediately killed when the hijackers forced their way into the cockpit. All that matters to me was that LeRoy did not suffer. The coroner had told me that everyone would have been unconscious because of the rapid depressurization of the plane; they would have been unconscious before the plane hit the ground. I left the Princeton hotel grateful for the truth.

9

AIRLINE SAFETY

"Billions of dollars have been spent addressing [the] screening of passengers and checked baggage, a larger force of Federal Air Marshals, and reinforced cockpit doors. And yet it is an undisputed fact that the system is still substantially porous, and single-point failures take place all too frequently. It does not take much imagination to see we are still vulnerable to more September 11-style attacks."

—Ellen Saracini, in her statement to Congress in support of arming pilots, August 25, 2004

My first flight after September 11 was in November 2001 when I flew to Los Angeles to attend the Flag Run. I had never had a fear of flying and still don't. What I found difficult was seeing the pilots walking through the airport in their uniforms with flight bags and luggage in tow. The voice in my head said, "Why couldn't it have been you?" I would watch them and wonder if they were married, if they had kids and whether they were as needed by their loved ones as I needed LeRoy. A few weeks before September 11, LeRoy had told me about a captain he had flown with who had an autistic son. His relationship with his wife was non-existent, but he didn't want to have to pay alimony and child support, so they still lived under the same roof, yet lived separate lives. I thought about this story many times after LeRoy died. This man was unhappy. *Why couldn't it have been him?*

I had always liked airports, even before meeting LeRoy. People seemed happy at the airport, excited to be going on vacation or reuniting with family and friends. When LeRoy and I were dating long distance, airports became even more special to me. But now, even all these years later, certain airports, like LAX, hold more meaning for me and are almost unbearable to be in. Most of the time I'm traveling with the children, so I'm distracted. But when I travel alone, I force myself not to look left into the cockpit when boarding because it reminds me of when I would hang out in the cockpit for a few minutes before takeoff while LeRoy was doing his checks.

I also can't look out the window at the first officer doing the walk around. As part of his preflight checklist, the first officer has to physically inspect the plane from the outside, by walking around the aircraft. I had seen LeRoy do this many times, and seeing someone else do the inspection always makes me cry. And then I imagine LeRoy telling me, with his special brand of humor, that the guy doing the walk-around in the cold should be the one crying, which makes me smile a little.

Although airport security has increased, at times some of the new rules have seemed arbitrary and others completely senseless. On some flights I would be able to carry Laurel through the metal detector in her Baby Bjorn infant carrier. Other times I would have to wake her up, take her out of the carrier, and place the fabric carrier through the x-ray machine. One time a screener called a supervisor over to check on a decorative pin that was on my diaper bag. The pin was made of plastic with no sharp point. It concerned me that this individual, who was responsible for my safety, needed a supervisor to determine whether a plastic diaper pin could be used as a weapon. The supervisor approved the pin, but I ended up throwing it away to eliminate any confusion in the future.

These inconsistencies frustrated me because I could see that the system that had failed LeRoy was still seriously flawed. The biggest indication of this was when I flew to San Francisco to complete LeRoy's flight in January of 2002. My parents had flown in from Canada to care for Laurel while I was away. When my dad arrived in New Jersey, he realized he had forgotten to bring extra razors. So he asked me to go to the drugstore to buy a few for him, and gave me an old razor so I would know exactly which kind to get. I purchased the new razors but forgot to take the old razor out of my purse. It wasn't until I was on board United Flight 81 (formerly United 93) and flying to San Francisco that I noticed the razor in my purse. I had gone through security at the exact same gate as the individuals who had boarded Flight 93. And even with an NBC affiliate camera crew in tow, who had been filming me for a story of my flight, no one had noticed the razor in my purse as it went through the x-ray machine.

Because Laurel and I traveled back and forth to my parents' home in Canada a lot, I contacted Air Canada to see if I could get some assistance. When LeRoy had been alive, it was much easier to manage car seats, diaper bags, and strollers, in addition to the usual baggage. But now it was just me. I wasn't asking for a lifetime of favors; I just needed help for a couple of years until she was older and could walk on her own. But Air Canada, which was the airline I flew most frequently with Laurel, could not offer any assistance unless I had a physical disability. No exceptions despite my situation.

But of course there were exceptions. I knew this because I had received special assistance on several occasions. Over the years, I had been asked to attend various events in LeRoy's honor. After a car dropped me off at the airport, a VIP escort would facilitate my check-in, take me to an airport lounge, and then accompany me to my gate. When I arrived at my destination, I would receive the same VIP service. On a couple of occasions, after arriving at our destination, all the passengers were instructed to remain seated and I was escorted off the plane directly from the Jetway to the tarmac where a limousine with a police escort was waiting to take me to my hotel. On another occasion, I was taken through the airport by an alternate route to avoid waiting media. I didn't want or need the attention or the VIP treatment. What I needed was simply a helping hand when I was traveling with my daughter. But since I was able-bodied and not an A-list celebrity, there was no help available.

I decided soon after September 11 that I would adopt a child. I didn't want Laurel to grow up without a sibling and I had always planned on having more children. LeRoy and I had discussed adoption even before we were married, and had decided that if we were unable to have children of our own, we would build our family this way instead. I started the adoption process in January 2003, knowing I needed that extra time to pull myself together before taking on the responsibility of a newborn. Alden was born in June 2004 and joined our family when he was just two days old.

It was difficult traveling with two kids. But I would grit my teeth and do it, trying not to cry in frustration as people would practically knock me over to get on and off the plane. Once, when my son was only a baby, I fell on the tarmac while carrying him. In order to prevent his head from hitting the asphalt, I reached my arm up to get my hand underneath the back of his head. There was an airline employee there who asked me if I was okay. My elbow and knee hurt but I said I was okay, and he went on his way. A few minutes later I looked down at my elbow. I had sheared the skin off; it was still attached but I was bleeding profusely. I approached a couple of gate agents, and then a couple of vendors in the food court, to see if anyone could locate a first aid kit. But no one could, and no one even offered to call someone to help me. Finally, a passenger who had overheard my attempts gave me several bandages she had in her purse. Once in a while someone would see me struggling to fold my stroller or to lift something into the overhead bins and would come to my rescue. But more often than not, we were on our own.

I figured out ways to travel without help. I wouldn't drink anything before or during the flights because I couldn't leave the kids and go to the bathroom. I carried a backpack instead of a purse, so my hands would be free. I bought extra car seats to keep at my parents' house, so I wouldn't have to carry them back and forth.

But we would often still run into a snag. I was checking in for an Air Canada flight, and as luck would have it, United Airlines and Air Canada are codeshare partners. Codeshare partnerships are an aviation business arrangement where two airlines share the same flight. At Philadelphia International Airport, the codeshare arrangement meant that when I flew with Air Canada, I had to check in with a United Airlines ticket agent. After arriving at the airport I waited in line for about forty-five minutes, as there were only a couple of ticket agents working the counter. When it was finally my turn, the agent told me the flight was closed and I would have to take the next flight, which was scheduled for five hours later. Even though the plane was at the gate, and wasn't scheduled to depart for another forty-five minutes, she did not anticipate me making it through security in time, and suggested that I should have arrived at the airport earlier.

No mention was made of the obvious lack of available ticket agents and the length of time I had waited in line with two children. I had arrived at the airport ninety minutes prior to our flight, which at the time was the requirement for a flight to Toronto. I was tired from all the packing and preparation I had done to get us to the airport on time. The day before had been my wedding anniversary and I was feeling more emotional than usual. I knew that if LeRoy had been with me with his employee identification badge, the agent would have called up to the gate to tell them to hold the door, and then a United employee would have escorted us upstairs to security to expedite the process. I knew this because it had happened before.

I broke down right at the counter, in front of the agents and their customers. I told them about LeRoy, how he had died for this airline on September 11, and that if he hadn't died working for this airline, I wouldn't have to travel by myself with two small children. I told them what I thought he would think about the lack of consideration they were showing me. And I told them I would not wait five hours until the next flight on Air Canada. They needed to put me on the next flight to Toronto. Fairly quickly, seats were arranged for us on a US Airways flight to Toronto, scheduled to depart within a couple of hours.

I was in Jamaica on vacation with my family when the 2006 London plot to blow up planes using liquid explosives was uncovered. The authorities had stopped a planned attack to blow up airplanes destined for North America. The plot involved several individuals who had planned to carry liquids on board planes, and then once airborne, the liquids would be combined to make bombs that would explode. During our vacation, my son had developed an infection in his foot; the resort physician prescribed two medications for my son, and both were liquids. When we went through security in Jamaica, they didn't know what to do about my son's medications. They wanted to know why the prescriptions were not labeled with my son's name. I explained that they had not been filled at a pharmacy but had been provided by a physician. No one seemed to know what to do, so we were allowed to board our flight.

I was relieved that we were able to return home, yet a little unsettled at how easy it had been to get around the new regulations, which had only been in place for a few days. The new rules and restrictions meant I wasn't allowed to bring my son's sippy cups on the plane anymore. However, the one time I forgot to remove juice boxes from my carry-on bag on a trip back to New Jersey that Christmas, no one noticed.

Each time a new safety measure has been put in place, it seems to only address the near misses. For example, thanks to Richard Reid, also referred to as the "shoe bomber," who attempted to blow up a commercial airplane in flight in December 2001, we are now required to take our shoes off when going through security. We now can carry only limited amounts of liquids in our carry-on luggage as a result of the 2006 transatlantic aircraft plot to detonate liquid explosives carried on board. As far as the security screeners go, they may be wearing new uniforms, but they don't seem to be much more qualified than their predecessors. An incident at the Philadelphia Airport a couple of years ago proved me correct in my assumption. As I stood in the security line, I placed my shoes, purse, and a small bottle of hand sanitizer in one of the gray plastic bins. The TSA worker scanned my tray, removed the hand sanitizer, and told me I had to have a bag for it.

"But I only have the one item," I explained.

She pointed behind her to the sign with the pictures of toiletries in plastic bags and said those were the regulations.

I tried again. "This is my only item," I said, "so I don't need a bag." But she shook her head. I asked to speak to a supervisor.

An older gentleman approached, and I asked him why I needed a bag when I was only carrying one item. He also pointed to the sign behind him. So I said, "Then why was I able to carry this same bottle of hand sanitizer to and from Atlanta last week without it being in a bag?"

"Well, it's like speeding," he said glibly. "Sometimes you get caught. . . "

I interrupted him in a voice shaking with anger. "This is the system that caused my husband to be killed on September 11, 2001, so I think it's very important for the rules to be consistent."

He cut me off. "Would you like to take this outside?"

And although I am 5'3" tall and 120 pounds, compared to his 6" feet and well over 200 pounds, had I not been traveling with my two young children, I would have liked to see what this particular TSA supervisor would have done if we had "take[n] it outside."

Instead, he took my hand sanitizer and threw it away.

After September 11, Ellen Saracini was a driving force for championing the legislation to allow commercial airline pilots to be armed with guns. In 2002, this legislation was passed and pilots now have a choice as to whether they are armed when they are in the cockpit. I entrust the flight crews with my safety, as I always have—not the airport security.

Above: LeRoy Homer, United States Air Force Academy cadet, class of 1987, 31st Squadron.

Below: Pilot training at Laughlin Air Force Base, Del Rio, Texas, 1988.

Above: As a captain in the United States Air Force, LeRoy was promoted to aircraft commander of the C-141 in 1991.

Below: The night LeRoy proposed, Valentine's Day 1997.

Above: LeRoy began working for United in May 1995.

Below: Our wedding day, May 1998.

Above: London, England. My last trip with LeRoy before Laurel's birth.
Below: Laurel gardening with daddy in the summer of 2001.

Above: LeRoy and Laurel in July 2001.

Below: Our last family photo, Labor Day 2001.

Above: Visiting the crash site for the first time in September 2002.

Below: Laurel wearing her dad's hat on the beach at Cape Canaveral, FL several hours before a Titan IV rocket, dedicated to LeRoy, takes off into space.

10

BROKEN PROMISES

"I, LeRoy Homer, having been appointed a Second Lieutenant in the United States Air Force, do solemnly swear that I will support and defend the Constitution of the United States against all enemies, foreign and domestic; that I will bear true faith and allegiance to the same; that I take this obligation freely, without any mental reservation or purpose of evasion; and that I will well and faithfully discharge the duties of the office upon which I am about to enter, so help me God."

—LeRoy Homer, United States Air Force
Oath of Commission, May 1987

Most of the family members of the crew avoided the media. However, immediately after the listening session for passengers' families had concluded, several individuals conducted media interviews despite the confidentiality agreement.

I couldn't help but see the irony in the situation. The very people who had been so greatly impacted by those who had disregarded our laws were now willing to do the same, and for what? Television appearances? Book deals? Dialogue in a Lisa Beamer book published a few months after we heard the recording was remarkably similar to what we had heard on the tape. I can only guess that for some, the personal notoriety and financial gains must have seemed worth the risk that Zacarias Moussaoui might benefit from their divulgence of confidential information, especially since there were no legal consequences for their actions. It was hard to imagine anyone feeling they had the right to make choices that could impact everyone who had lost a loved one on any of those flights.

As a nurse, I take confidentiality seriously. I couldn't understand how these individuals could ignore the agreement they had signed in such an overt manner. When I contacted Dave Novak, the U.S. Assistant District Attorney, about this matter, he agreed that it was not judicious for individuals to breach the agreement; however, the government would not be taking any action against them because they were seen as victims. He suggested I take my concerns directly to the individuals. An e-mail group had started within months of September 11 as a way for family members to receive information. On September 4, 2002, I sent the following e-mail to the family members of Flight 93:

I would like to address a concern I discussed today with Dave Novak, U.S. Assistant District Attorney. Those of us who chose to listen to the CVR signed confidentiality agreements; however, it appears that many people have chosen to disregard that. Not only is this legally and ethically irresponsible, it invades the rights of those family members who chose not to participate. It is disgusting to me that people would break an agreement to increase their celebrity or profit financially. Not only are they jeopardizing the criminal case against someone who is responsible for the loss of our loved ones, they are also ignoring the additional pain this may be causing families who may inadvertently see an interview on television or read a press release about books that are being published. I am fortunate that my daughter is not old enough to understand and be subjected to this. The actions of our family members on that plane who acted out of concern for "the greater good" are being made a mockery by this "what's in it for me" attitude. We expect others to respect the laws of our country when many of us cannot even honor a simple confidentiality agreement.

Mr. Novak is very concerned with what has happened, and as a result has indicated that no more information will be shared with the families prior to the trial because of the lack of restraint shown after the CVR hearing. He also informed me that the government is unwilling to address the individuals involved because they are already seen as victims, and the perception would be that now they are being additionally hurt by the government. He did think that if the family members who are unhappy with the breach of information were to make their feelings known, it may be helpful in stopping the continuous hurtful nature of these disclosures. Obviously, what has already been said is out there; books have already been written. We can, however, decide to prevent this from continuing.

I received numerous e-mail messages from family members thanking me for saying what they had also been thinking and feeling. I also received an e-mail from one of the individuals who had written a book denying she had written anything she had heard on the cockpit voice recorder; she stated that "anything contained in her book was gathered from public information which had already been published in a variety of sources." Much of the information elicited from these interviews was interpreted in ways which could not be proven. For example, sounds of dishes slamming against each other turned into the idea that a food cart had been used to ram open the cockpit door. Once this was repeated a few times, it became a part of the story. I had flown on a Boeing 757 and knew there were twelve seats in first class; the first two rows had four seats with the aisle in the middle; the third and fourth rows were only on the left side of the plane with the galley to the right. The idea of men described as "burly" and "athletic" maneuvering a food cart single file through a narrow aisle of this airplane in order to break into the cockpit was absurd.

One of the main problems with the security of the cockpit prior to September 11 was the inherent weakness of the cockpit doors. With the carts never having been secured after breakfast because of the takeover of the plane, the sounds of dishes breaking was likely due to the pitches and rolls of the airplane that had been recorded on the flight data recorder. But fiction became fact when these comments were published in *Among the Heroes,* which included the author's interviews with family members after they had heard the recording. Ultimately, *The 9/11 Commission Report* proved the passengers had never made it to the cockpit, but by the time the report was completed, *Among the Heroes,* the first book published about Flight 93, had become a reputable source of information.

I heard an interesting radio interview a while ago

on media reporting. Scott R. Maier, a journalism professor at the University of Oregon, had done research on media errors; after identifying over 1200 factual errors in news stories, he discovered that 98 percent of these errors went uncorrected. These errors would be perpetuated when other journalists used inaccurate information from the same news stories without doing their own investigation. So although information in *Among the Heroes* would eventually be disproved, the book became *the* source for information, at least until *The 9/11 Commission Report* was published in 2004, providing a more accurate portrayal of what had happened on Flight 93.

In the fall of 2005, I was contacted by Universal Studios. I had heard the rumors, and evidently they were true: a feature film was being made about Flight 93. I agreed to speak with the producer, despite my misgivings, because I knew the film would be made whether or not I participated. When I spoke with the producer, Kate Solomon, I was as guarded as I had learned to be with the media. Yet her sincerity, coupled with her British accent, had already started to win me over even before we met face to face.

A few things stood out during our meeting at a local coffee shop. Dressed casually and wearing no makeup, Kate seemed very down to earth. She was a real person and a great listener. I immediately liked her. She told me how the project had come about, and how deeply the director, Paul Greengrass, had been affected by September 11 and LeRoy's flight in particular. After the London bombings that summer, Greengrass had felt strongly that the story of Flight 93 should be told. He characterized it as the story of the flight that fought back, as the first strike against the terrorist attacks. The film wouldn't be a big budget production and there wouldn't be any big name movie stars. As I listened, I knew that if someone was going to make this film, I wanted it to be Paul Greengrass.

Kate interviewed me for several hours that day. We talked about LeRoy and what kind of person he was, both at home and at work. She wanted to know as much about him as possible to help with casting. A few of the little details I had shared with her made it on screen, like the fact that a lot of pilots carry hot sauce in their flight bags to spice up their crew meals. I loved talking about LeRoy and Kate seemed to enjoy hearing about him. When we talked about that day, I told her my story. But there were still many details I was not allowed to divulge because the Moussaoui trial was still pending and I was bound by the confidentiality agreement. What I did tell her was about LeRoy's years of experience. LeRoy had achieved the rank of major in 1999, and received commendations for his service in Desert Shield and Desert Storm. He had also received recognition for his humanitarian missions to Somalia, where he had flown relief supplies into hostile territory in 1993.

I had hoped to have an opportunity to share all the information I had about the flight. After years of delays, the trial was scheduled to start within months. But Kate explained the filming would take place in the next couple of months over a six-week period and would likely be completed before the trial was over.

The actual CVR was sealed after the Moussaoui trial; the judge allowed only the transcripts of the CVR to be released. Some of the Flight 93 family members who pursued lawsuits against United Airlines, Boeing (the airplane's manufacturer), and Argenbright Security attempted to have the judge release the actual recording, arguing that the transcript did not accurately portray what the people aboard the flight had endured. To my knowledge, none of the families of people heard on the recording were involved in the lawsuit. I could only assume the reason to have the recording would be for its shock value, which could increase the amount the jury would award to the families. But again, it seemed that no thought was given to the other families' rights for privacy.

I had experienced the horror of hearing the air traffic control tapes played on television. The ATC recording, which can be accessed on the Internet, may one day be discovered by my daughter. Did the people who were adamant in wanting the recording to be played think it was appropriate to listen to their loved ones begging, pleading, fighting for their lives? Had they even considered the effects on the other family members, especially the children of the crew members? Fortunately, the suit was settled. The same individuals who had wanted their "day in court to have the truth finally come out" settled for an undisclosed amount.

It has been interesting to see the dynamics among the Flight 93 family members play out over the years. A hierarchy developed quickly. The four passenger heroes—Todd Beamer, Tom Burnett, Jeremy Glick, and Mark Bingham—were at the top, presumably because of the media broadcasting the phone calls they had made to their family members. Everyone else on board was made less significant in what had transpired on the flight. When *The 9/11 Commission Report* was released, I discovered there had been many calls made that we had not been aware of, because the families had chosen not to publicize them. While most of the family members seemed to want to deal with their grief as privately as possible, others seemed to embrace the attention.

Although I have never met Lisa Beamer, I saw her on television several times promoting the foundation she started within days of September 11. According to the Associated Press on October 20, 2001, The Todd M. Beamer Memorial Foundation was created to provide for "the 22 children that lost a parent on Flight 93." It was never made clear exactly how these funds would be distributed or used. Although my daughter, one of the twenty-two children, was being used essentially as a fundraising tool, I was never contacted by anyone from the foundation.

A couple years later, the Associated Press reported that The Todd M. Beamer Foundation's name had changed to Heroic Choices, a program that would aid children ages eight to twelve who lost a parent on September 11, as well as youngsters who have been sexually assaulted, come from an abusive home, or have a parent in prison. The program would be offered in the immediate New York City area. Since the funds raised would now go to any child faced with a trauma, not just children who had lost a parent on Flight 93, and given we did not live in New York, it seemed unlikely that Laurel would be eligible for any program this new organization would offer. It was reported in the article that Heroic Choices had raised over $4.5 million in donations in the years immediately after 2001, but by 2007, the *NonProfit Times* reported that the foundation's most recent IRS Form 990 showed only $177,539 in assets. Later that year, Heroic Choices closed its doors, shut down its website, and disconnected its phones. While I have not been in contact with all twenty-two children, and perhaps some children did receive assistance, of the children I know personally, none of them have benefitted from this foundation. There is no record of how that money was spent, but it was not used for the purpose for which it was raised.

11

FIRST ANNIVERSARY

"You know the plans You have for me, O Lord. You have declared that
they are plans to prosper me and not to harm me, plans to give me
a hope and a future."

—Jeremiah 29:11

On the first anniversary of September 11, I made my first visit to Shanksville, Pennsylvania. I had never received an invitation to attend the memorial service held on September 18, 2001, at which First Lady Laura Bush and then-Governor Tom Ridge presided. The Flight 93 family members were invited, yet I was somehow overlooked. Even if I had been invited, I doubt I would have attended given my state of mind at the time.

During the past year I had seen no reason to visit Shanksville. What would I gain by seeing the place where my husband had died? As far as I was concerned, it was a place where something bad had happened, and I couldn't imagine that going there would do me any good. But as the one-year anniversary approached, I decided to attend the planned events honoring the Flight 93 crew and its passengers. I knew Sandy would be there as well as some of the other family members I had met during the year. Being with other people who had experienced such a similar loss might be comforting. The Network of Victim Assistance (NOVA), the agency assigned to assist the families of Flight 93 victims, had coordinated our travel and accommodations for the anniversary events. I still wasn't comfortable driving long distances by myself, especially with Laurel, who was now a toddler. Arrangements were made for me to travel by train to Johnstown, Pennsylvania, the closest train station, about thirty miles from Shanksville; from there, I would be driven to the lodge where the Flight 93 family members were staying.

Before I could leave for Shanksville, I had an event I needed to attend closer to home. On September 8, 2002, I attended a dedication for "Memorial Walk," a memorial garden that had been built in the town where we lived to honor LeRoy. When Chris Medvec, a local Boy Scout, learned that LeRoy had been the first officer of United 93, he decided to build a memorial honoring LeRoy for his Eagle Scout project. Chris solicited contractors to design, build, and donate materials for the memorial. The design would feature a large rock in the center of the garden, with a bronze plaque mounted on the side. Chris asked me to choose the wording for the plaque. It reads: "LeRoy Homer, September 11, 2001. First Officer, Flight 93. Husband, Father, Friend. 'Greater love hath no man than this, that a man would lay down his life for his friends.' "

I was pleased with how the memorial turned out. Evergreens formed a semi-circle around the garden, making the memorial feel private and separate from the activities going on around it. A small wooden bench was placed in the center, where I have sat on my visits over the years. I was humbled by the generosity of the community. When I stood to thank Chris and everyone who had been involved in making the memorial a reality, I used the opportunity to thank all the people who had helped me get through the past year. My neighbors had never stopped bringing us meals. The guy who operated the garbage truck stopped and got out of his truck every week to wheel my trash can to the garage. My mailman, Chuck, also got out of his truck more than he had to, bringing my mail up to the door, always with a smile and a few words of encouragement. I thanked Chris, the guy at FedEx, who LeRoy and I had gotten to know over the years. When I had gone in to mail packages, he gave me his FedEx discount, knowing I no longer had the discount through the airline. The members of this community had taken good care of me, and I used this opportunity to thank them. The next day I left for Shanksville.

My parents, my brother and sister-in-law, and my aunt drove from Canada to be in Shanksville with me for the anniversary. My sister flew in from Georgia. Most of LeRoy's family was there as well. Seeing their familiar faces helped with the stress and anxiety I had been feeling on the train ride. There was an itinerary of events planned for the two days the families would be in Shanksville, enough activity to propel me through my time there.

My biggest fear as September 11, 2002 drew closer was the weather. I remembered the weather on Tuesday, September 11, 2001 very clearly: the clear blue sky, the smell of the air, the feel of it on my skin. I knew if the weather was at all similar one year later, it would feel like I had been pulled back into the nightmare. Years later I would understand that this fear was related to my post-traumatic stress disorder (PTSD). Fortunately, the weather on September 11, 2002 was as opposite as it could possibly be. It was an overcast, blustery, cold day—so cold, in fact, that blankets were passed out during the outdoor ceremony.

President Bush and the First Lady had also come to

Shanksville to lay a wreath at the crash site and to meet with the family members. My feelings towards the president were conflicted. President Bush had received a daily presidential briefing in early August, warning him of attacks. The FBI had already known about Zacharias Moussaoui who had raised suspicion when it was discovered after he was arrested for an immigration violation that he had been taking flight lessons. Many people who I had spoken to that year who worked for the government or the military had told me the system was "blinking red" all summer; there had been "a lot of chatter." I took this to mean that the government knew there was an imminent threat. Was there more Bush could have done to prevent September 11?

What concerned me the most was the president's insistence that there did not need to be public inquiries into what had gone wrong. I have never met Kristen Breitweiser, Patty Casazza, Mindy Kleinberg, and Lorie van Auken, the four women who became widows on September 11 when their husbands who worked in the Twin Towers were killed. These women who called themselves "the Jersey Girls" fought tirelessly for a public investigation into what had led to September 11. After months of pleading their case for a public inquiry along with their many supporters, the 9/11 Commission was eventually created to investigate the events leading up to September 11, as well as what transpired during that day. If it weren't for them, there may have never been a 9/11 Commission, and I was thankful they were doing a job that many of us would have done had we had the energy and wherewithal.

All of this was on my mind that day and I really had no desire to meet the president or have a photograph taken by the White House photographers. But one of my sisters-in-law suggested Laurel might someday want to have a picture of her with the president. So I waited as the president and Mrs. Bush made their way to each family member, taking pictures and shaking hands.

When the president shook my hand, I said nothing. I didn't introduce myself and he didn't know who I was; I doubted that the fact my husband had been one of the pilots was of any importance to him. The president had singled out Lisa Beamer, who had been invited to the U.S. Capitol to hear President Bush in his first speech to Congress after the attacks. The President had even used the "Let's roll!" phrase in his address, reported to have been said by Todd Beamer, as a rallying cry against terrorism. I, on the other hand, had received a preprinted condolence card sometime in early 2002. I couldn't help thinking that the president should have been able to send out forty personally signed condolence cards to the families of the individuals on board Flight 93, frequently referred to by the media as "the flight of heroes." The card I had received was meaningless.

Pictures were taken, and the president moved on. Most people waited for the president as he moved along greeting each family; others were seeking out Condoleezza Rice and other government officials who were also in attendance, attempting to get as many photos as possible. The feeling of reverence was broken—some people only seemed to be concerned with having their picture taken with each of the VIPs. I felt physically ill; it felt like people were dancing in a graveyard, temporarily forgetting where we were standing. I have not since returned to the crash site.

12

HITTING BOTTOM

*"If you see a man drowning, do you ask him to call you sometime
if you need help? You just jump in."*

—Linda Feinberg, *I'm Grieving as Fast as I Can*

After I returned home from Shanksville, I fell apart.
All the feelings I had been holding in—shock and
disbelief, grief and regret—overwhelmed me. My
doctor had been trying various combinations of antidepressants to address my ongoing physical problems,
such as the twitching that occurred when I became
anxious, as well as my psychological issues. I still had
trouble falling asleep, although the nightmares had
decreased and I now slept through the night. Yet I still
had trouble concentrating.

The most difficult change for me to deal with was
my short-term memory impairment. Everything had
to be written down, not just things that needed to be

done, but also things that had already been done. I would have lengthy conversations and then have no recollection of those conversations a day or a week later. Even when reminded of comments I had made, I often felt like I was hearing the conversation for the first time. This was extremely distressing, because it happened virtually overnight—one day my memory was fine, and the next day I couldn't recall simple things. My day-to-day routine now required more planning. I rarely remembered the date. Sometimes my guess would be several days off. When my doctor asked me my age during an appointment, I couldn't remember at first. I knew the year of my birthday but I was having a hard time remembering the current year.

And I was always bone-tired. I was raising a child and had returned to work, so being tired may have been normal, except that I was tired all the time, regardless of how much sleep I got. I had always known LeRoy was a source of energy for me. Don't get me wrong, I had also been self-motivated. After all, I put myself through graduate school, working full-time night shifts to pay for it. But LeRoy, my biggest cheerleader, gave me the energy to take care of our family and our home, and still pursue my career. Now that source of energy was gone.

As much as I could, I had allowed the constant activity of looking after Laurel to distract me. I had spent a year trying to hold my feelings in. I didn't want my family to see me crying if I could help it. They were dealing with their own pain. And I didn't want them to worry about me any more than they already did. I couldn't cry at work, and I tried not to cry too much in front of Laurel. I did most of my crying during weekly therapy sessions or at my doctor's office, as he continued to try me on different combinations of antidepressants and anxiety medications. I had been having frequent panic attacks usually triggered by something I would unexpectedly see or hear in the newspaper or on television. It seemed there would be a September 11 headline every time I signed on to my computer to retrieve my e-mail.

People would often tell me that LeRoy was in a better place, watching over Laurel and me. I had even received a letter from a woman who claimed LeRoy had made contact with her; she dictated a letter to be given to me. The letter was very disturbing. It was written as if LeRoy were speaking to me and Laurel. The sentiments were generic, that he saw me crying at the edge of my bed at night and that he was watching over us. As much as I knew all these people meant well, none of this was helpful, and I didn't appreciate having the beliefs of others—some of who were total strangers—forced on me.

I knew they all meant well, but I would have

preferred not to listen to everyone's version of the afterlife. I believed in God and eternal life, but the beliefs of the Seventh-day Adventist church differ in some ways from most other Protestant religions. We believe in the Advent, which is the second coming of Jesus Christ. Those who have died will remain in their graves until the second coming. Then, our loved ones will be raised from the dead and we will go to Heaven with them, where we will live for eternity. So although I believed LeRoy was not in Heaven trying to communicate with me, I have always believed in an eternity and in a Heaven where I will be reunited with LeRoy.

Society does not allow much time for grieving, and I was trailing behind. It was only a few months after LeRoy's death when people started suggesting I needed to get out. Well-meaning friends and even people meeting me for the first time would sometimes ask if I had met anyone yet. What about online dating? I hadn't taken the usual actions to show I had accepted my loss. I had not disposed of LeRoy's clothes, his voice was still on our answering machine, and his name was still on our checks. I still wore my wedding band because I didn't know how to make myself feel not married. Neither LeRoy nor I believed in divorce. I had planned to spend the rest of my life with him, to grow old with him, "until death do us part." And I wasn't dead.

I was asked by my friends and even by my therapist if I felt I was betraying LeRoy by not moving on, as though I had made a choice to be devastated by a reality I could not yet comprehend. My husband's plane had been hijacked and crashed into the ground at such a velocity that there was no body to recover. LeRoy was never coming home. In a split second, all the plans we had made for the future were erased, and I was left to raise our child by myself. I had not made a choice. I was devastated; my life had been shattered and destroyed.

I missed LeRoy horribly, in so many different ways. I stopped watching our favorite television shows. I missed being a wife, taking care of someone. I had enjoyed cooking for LeRoy because he always made me feel like I was the best cook in the world. I missed cuddling with him at night. Many times, even years later, I woke up wanting to tell LeRoy something, and then I would remember.

One day I was driving home from work and realized I wouldn't be able to feel his ears when I kissed him ever again. LeRoy had a great sense of humor, and was always cracking me up. Sometimes I would think of something funny he had said or a joke we had shared. I would laugh out loud and then I would start to cry. I was hit with the realization many times during the first year after losing LeRoy that this was the way it would be from now on. I felt like I was drowning and I didn't have the emotional or physical energy to stay afloat.

What no one realized—myself included—was that I had been in shock for an entire year. I couldn't get my mind around what had happened. The pain was too intense to deal with, so I had blocked everything out as best I could. I only talked about LeRoy in the present, and never used the word "died." I would say "before everything happened" and "after everything happened" to avoid using the "D" word.

I had been back to work for almost a year. My job entailed presenting information on symptoms of cancer treatment to health care professionals at hospitals, doctors' offices, professional nursing organizations, and support groups. I spoke with small groups and to larger audiences at cancer symposiums. I had thought work would be the one place where I could have some normalcy. But even work was different. I could tell I made people feel uncomfortable just from my presence. No one knew what to say to me, except for the oncology nurses I worked with who were accustomed to having difficult conversations with their patients. These nurses were not afraid to talk to me about my significant weight loss, to ask about my medications, or to suggest different types of therapy. I felt comfortable with them and could tell them the truth about how I felt.

It became more and more difficult to do my job. My voice was becoming shaky, and I had trouble getting my words out. I couldn't recall simple words I had used countless times before. Since my job involved public speaking, it became increasingly difficult to conduct my lectures. It soon became obvious that the distraction of work was not helping me, and now a job I had once enjoyed had become stressful because of my trauma's cognitive effects on my memory and speech.

I continued with the plans we had made for Laurel. I bought a piano and signed Laurel up for lessons. I signed her up for swim lessons and dance, too. I took her to Disneyland and to her first concert, *Barney and Friends*, but had no interest in what was going on around me because of the excruciating pain I felt. I couldn't imagine how I would be able to stand such pain for the remainder of my life. I had heard stories about the husband or wife who dies within months or even weeks of the death of their partner. Even though I had only heard of these occasions of "dying of a broken heart" happening with older couples, I was sometimes surprised my own heart hadn't stopped. For many years to come, there would be days I didn't think would end. I longed for the escape of night and sleep. "The days are long and the years are short" was a saying that rang true.

During that first year, I was preoccupied with all the items that needed to be resolved. The paperwork was monumental. I canceled LeRoy's driver's license and credit cards, changed the names on all our accounts, and filled out paperwork for the airline and the military, as well as for NOVA, the Red Cross, United Way, and several other agencies, many of which were providing help to victims' families. I needed to fill out forms for social security benefits; settle LeRoy's estate; apply for disability insurance in case I was injured while at work; and set up a new will, since I was now Laurel's sole provider. The Canadian Consulate in New York provided me with the letter I would need to carry when I traveled with Laurel out of the country, explaining why I was traveling with her unaccompanied by her father. Every day it seemed I was faced with a new task or responsibility.

After that first year, as the shock wore off, reality set in. Within six months of my visit to Shanksville, I had lost another ten pounds. Before September 11, I had been a size 4; a few months later I was a size 0. Ellen and I joked about starting a September 11 "Widows Clothing Line" that would carry only sizes 0-2. I continued to lose weight, to the point that I was wearing clothes from the juniors department. Sometimes I would forget to eat, and nothing tasted good anyway. I knew I wasn't taking care of myself. I was still having problems with my memory. So much had happened in such a short amount of time, I hadn't been able to process it all. Several of the pilots who came to LeRoy's memorial service had to be introduced more than once. This happened not only at LeRoy's memorials, but on the first anniversary in Shanksville. My mind wandered a lot, and I found that I had to write things down. I had always been a list maker, and now I was making lists with tasks like remembering to take pictures of Laurel. I had developed a twitch in my left foot, which would sometimes go away with my anti-anxiety medication, but if I was really stressed, the twitching would spread from my foot upwards until my entire body was affected.

The weekends seemed endless because I didn't have the distractions of work and errands like I did during the week. I would watch the clock to see how many more hours I had before I could put Laurel to bed so that I could take an Ambien and escape for another night. Sundays had been my favorite day in my "before everything happened" life. On Sundays, LeRoy and I would debate whose turn it was to go get the bagels and the newspaper. The rest of the day would be spent outside gardening or lounging on the porch, or we might take a day trip to New Hope, Pennsylvania or Fairmount Park in Philadelphia. After

Laurel was born, LeRoy would get up on Sunday and feed her breakfast so I could sleep in. But now, by Sunday night I was physically and emotionally exhausted from the demands of caring for Laurel by myself. I kept LeRoy's Swiss Army knife, the one he should have had with him on September 11, in the drawer of my nightstand. Sometimes I would use it to make scratches on my skin. The crushing pain in my chest would then shift to wherever I had scratched myself and I would feel temporary relief.

I missed the sound of the garage door opening late at night, a sound that let me know LeRoy was home safely from a trip. The pictures of LeRoy were still where they had been the year before, except now I couldn't look at them. When I looked at a picture of us together, I almost didn't recognize myself. I looked so happy and unaware, so naïve. *That girl has no clue*, I would think.

When I wasn't out presenting a lecture or in a meeting, I was working out of my home office; I spent a lot of time alone. When I did go out to do errands after September 11, I would sometimes experience panic attacks. If too many people were in a store, I would have to leave. Sometimes hearing a certain song that would remind me of LeRoy would be enough to send me running out to my car. Every once in a while someone would recognize me or recognize my name on my credit card. I would see their eyes fill up with tears; perhaps it was empathy, but I would feel like my presence had ruined part of their day. I remember picking up Laurel from Digna's one evening. As I crossed the street, another parent was picking up his child. He must have recognized me because he walked up to me in front of Digna's house and, after extending his condolences, asked if I had heard the cockpit voice recording yet.

The question, "How are you doing?" was never easy to answer because if I told the truth, I would be reduced to tears, and in most cases I knew the person asking didn't really want the truth. They wanted me to be fine, which I wasn't. My standard response to those who knew me became "One day closer to my death," always delivered in an upbeat voice. No one seemed sure what to say after that. An appropriate answer, I thought, to an absurd question.

Many people told me, "You're young, you'll meet someone else," mostly people who after finding out who I was, couldn't conceivably think of anything else to say. To me this remark suggested that my husband, someone I loved more than anything, was easily replaceable. I was twenty-nine when I met LeRoy, and he was thirty. It had taken us awhile to find each other. I knew someone like LeRoy didn't come along very often. Some people live their entire lives not ever experiencing the contentment and happiness I had shared with LeRoy. He had made me a better person. He was my husband and my family. The fact that he was no longer alive did not change any of that.

"LeRoy would want you to be happy," was another sentiment I heard far too many times. I wanted to be happy, too. But the person I needed to make me happy had been taken from me.

As the months went by, I continued to experience my loss in different ways. After September 11, United Airlines seemed to distance themselves from me as well as from the other United Airlines families. Even after we had resolved the majority of issues with the company, it became more difficult to try to get through to someone at United when we had a concern or problem. Ellen, Sandy, Miriam, and I had all experienced situations with various departments at United—benefits, travel, and pension—with varying degrees of frustration. We were eventually assigned a single point of contact within United to help us navigate the different departments, which helped to a certain extent.

The U.S. Air Force revoked my military ID due to LeRoy's death, so I could no longer go on base. We had done a lot of our grocery shopping there when LeRoy was alive. My mail started to come addressed to Ms. instead of Mrs. When the "In Case of Emergency" information needed to be filled out on my medical forms, it was yet another reminder that I was now alone. Sure, I could list my brother, sister, or parents. But I didn't want to. LeRoy and I were a team. We took care of each other. Now I was on my own.

13

GETTING HELP

"They say time heals everything, but I'm still waiting."

—The Dixie Chicks, "Taking the Long Way Around"

Although I had been diagnosed with PTSD and MDD (major depressive disorder) in 2001 by my family physician, in 2002 I was sent to Steven Perkel, DSW, of the American Academy of Experts in Traumatic Stress for a more thorough evaluation:

> "Melodie Homer has had several injuries directly related to the death of her husband, the manner in which he died, and the events that have occurred subsequently. The death of LeRoy Homer and the manner in which it occurred, as well as the high visibility, have been injurious.

It is also important to note that Mrs. Homer reports having been told that her husband was safe by his employer, only to find out moments later by watching CNN that Flight 93 had crashed in Pennsylvania. At the time, she was alone at home with her infant daughter and was emotionally damaged by learning of her husband's death via television. Additionally, the fact that Mr. Homer's flight was hijacked by terrorists and that this was an intentional act to harm the crew and passengers of Flight 93 increased the impact of the trauma and was an additional injury. Mrs. Homer has had extended exposure to the traumatic events of September 11 resulting in more complex and grievous emotional injuries. This is consistent with the literature on the impact of Type II traumatic events, those that involve prolonged exposure to stressors. Type II exposures are more likely to inflict greater psychological damage than acute Type I single, un-prolonged exposures.

Mrs. Homer has the classic symptoms of Post-traumatic Stress Disorder and is currently receiving treatment for this disorder. Her view of the future is pessimistic and she is searching for meaning in her life while

> coping with the void left by her
> husband's violent and highly visible
> death. Given the length of exposure
> and the ongoing investigation and the
> war on terrorism, Mrs. Homer
> continues to be subjected to significant
> stressors."

I started seeing a psychologist in October 2001 who was experienced in dealing with people who had witnessed traumatic deaths; most of his patients were police officers and veterans. I attended weekly sessions for several months. The psychologist's main concerns were my ability to function, the medications I was taking, and the risk for dependence on Valium, which I was taking for anxiety, and Ambien. He encouraged me to try relaxation techniques as an alternative to medication. After several weeks, he declared me functional. By this time I had returned to work, and as I was caring for Laurel and myself, I was released from his care. In retrospect, I wasn't ready to go back to work in November 2001. But I didn't know what else to do besides returning to what I had been doing. Being at work allowed me to keep my professional identity. I had lost so much of myself already; I couldn't stand to lose more.

Most of the time, I didn't even feel like I was living in the same place as everyone else. While I was awake, I was living completely in my head, in my former life, in my memories. I felt like there was also a room in my head, a room where I was keeping all the information I didn't want to approach. I later learned the term for this: disassociating. It took all my energy to keep the door to this room closed, but sometimes, when I was overwhelmed in one way or another, that door would fly wide open. In that excruciating moment, I would have to think about what had happened to LeRoy and to my own life. Although outwardly, I appeared to be functioning, I still knew I was in desperate need of help.

I found another therapist, Debbie Feldman, in early 2002 who, unlike the previous therapists, dealt primarily with people suffering from profound grief. Over the course of two years, she would teach me ways to cope with situations that the new life I had been thrown into presented. Each week I would sit in her office and cry. There would always be some part of it that I would struggle with—an upcoming anniversary, my feelings of loneliness, hopelessness about the future. She helped me focus my energy when I felt pulled in too many directions. Therapy and my own reading helped me understand why my loss was so difficult and intense. There hadn't been a body. LeRoy left for work, just like he had many other mornings, and I never saw him again. I had experienced a sudden, unexpected loss, with no chance to let him know how much I loved him.

My therapist helped me understand why people interacted with me differently, why they said that LeRoy was in a better place or that I was young and would remarry—even the person who had asked about the cockpit voice recording. Once people found out who I was, they would want to hug me. I didn't enjoy being hugged by strangers, and instead of feeling comforted I started to feel like something was being taken from me or that I was obligated to comfort them. I was able to understand, with Debbie's help, that in most cases, people wanted a connection to September 11, perhaps in their own attempt to understand or make sense of the events.

When I would attend an event in LeRoy's honor, my stress level increased with the inevitability of being forced into a situation with strangers who felt they knew me because they had heard LeRoy's story or seen my picture in the newspaper or on television. I had become jumpy, and would startle in an exaggerated way in everyday situations. There were times when I was even startled by someone I had known was in the room with me the whole time. My body would react as if I was in danger—I would scream or pull away or drop whatever I was holding.

I had irrational thoughts. If I saw an armored car at the bank, I was sure it was going to be robbed while I was there. I saw suspicious-looking people everywhere.

I had all the symptoms of PTSD and major depression, and felt detached from everyone, even my own child. I couldn't perceive any type of future in which I'd be happy again.

After two years of therapy with Debbie, I had ways to cope with my new reality, but the pain was still as intense as it had ever been. Convinced my body wouldn't be able to handle my pain, I wrote out instructions for Laurel. I had already drawn up a new will. But there were other things that didn't belong in a will—plans LeRoy and I had made for her—and I wanted to make sure she would be taken care of the way we had planned. We wanted her to take swimming lessons. Non-negotiable. We also wanted her to have the opportunity to play a musical instrument. LeRoy had wanted to take piano lessons with Laurel when she was old enough. We wanted her to be raised going to church, being taught the same values we had been brought up with. We didn't want her to get every toy or gadget she asked for. I typed everything up on my computer and saved it on a disk, titled *Laurel.*

14

LAUREL

"When I cry, Laurel, my tears are not only for myself and LeRoy; they are also for you. I know that at best you will have vague memories and recollections of your father. I know that the only way you will be able to remember him is through the stories you hear and pictures others will paint for you. I feel guilty because I have something that you will never, ever experience . . . a father. I cry because LeRoy will never have a chance to teach you how to ride a bike, or the opportunity to walk you down the aisle on your wedding day. I cry for everything you will never have. My promise to you, Laurel, is that I will do my best to make sure you know what a wonderful man your father was. I will tell you how he cried the day you were born and how happy and proud he was. I will constantly tell you how much Daddy loved you."

—Excerpt from a 2002 letter to Laurel,
written by her Aunt Heather

Although Laurel only had her dad in her life for ten months, they had a special relationship. LeRoy was so excited to become a dad. He read two parenting books before she was born, and then continued to read after, wanting to anticipate what her next milestone would be. We both decided we would read a book to our unborn baby, and I picked *Harold's Purple Crayon,* one of the first books I can remember from my childhood. LeRoy decided on *Green Eggs and Ham*, and read it to our unborn baby every night he was home.

When my due date came and went, he started giving my belly pep talks, telling the baby we wanted to meet him or her and it was time to come out. We wanted the baby's gender to be a surprise, and even though LeRoy kept saying he wanted a boy, I knew as soon as Laurel was born that she would probably get a pony if she only asked her dad for one. He was smitten. Most of the video of Laurel's first months of life was recorded by LeRoy—you can hear him talking to her in the background, explaining things to her, or trying to get her to do something for the camera. I remember once when she was only a couple of weeks old, LeRoy had just come home from flying a London trip. He was always tired from those trips because of the time change. Laurel had been fussy that day and I was exhausted. I woke up at some point during the night and went to look for them. There they were, LeRoy sitting in the glider, looking exhausted but awake, Laurel asleep on her dad's lap. I never doubted he would be a wonderful father. It was the tenderness he shared with her that was so beautiful to watch.

LeRoy would pick Laurel up at daycare as soon as he got back from the airport. If I was on my way home from work, he would still pick her up. He wouldn't even go home to change first. When he was away and would call home, he would have me put the phone receiver up to her ear, so he could talk to her. When he was home, working in the office or on the computer, he rolled the bassinet right up next to his desk. When she got a little older, he would wear the baby carrier with her in it while he worked. When she got too big for the carrier, he moved her swing into the office. If he was out working in the garden, he would bring the ExerSaucer outside, so she could be next to him as he worked. He was incredibly creative at finding ways to keep her nearby.

Before Laurel was born, LeRoy told me he wanted to be involved in all of her care; he would just need me to show him what to do. He kept his word, changing her diapers and giving her baths. Sometimes I would hear him imitating funny voices when he was feeding her. He had the "Elmo's World" theme song memorized, and would make her giggle when he sang it to her with his dead-on Elmo impression. One night LeRoy decided he was going to demonstrate for Laurel how to crawl. He got down on the floor in front of her, trying to get her to follow behind. Laurel just sat there and giggled at him.

As amazing as I knew LeRoy was, he still managed to surprise me. In July 2001, I had gone to Chicago for a five-day work meeting. I had already traveled for work earlier in the year, and since I was breastfeeding at the time, LeRoy and Laurel had come with me to San Francisco. LeRoy had taken care of three-month-old Laurel in our hotel room while I attended meetings, slipping back to the room every few hours to nurse.

My Chicago trip was going to be from Monday to Friday, the longest I had been away from Laurel since she was born. I missed my baby, but the non-stop pace of the meetings didn't allow me much time to brood. On Tuesday when LeRoy called, he said he had decided they were going to come and spend the rest of the week with me. All he needed was for me to make him a list of what to pack for Laurel. When he arrived at the hotel in Chicago, having traveled with an eight-month-old all by himself, he had packed every item on the list. I imagine most men wouldn't know the difference between a onesie and a sleeper. But LeRoy knew.

Over the years, sometimes people would comment on the fact that since Laurel was only ten months old when she lost her dad, perhaps it would be easier for her to adjust to the loss. But almost immediately, Laurel showed signs that she sensed something was different. For the first few months after September 11, she would wake up with night terrors. Laurel had been sleeping through the night since she was three months old, so waking up at night was unusual for her. When I would pick her up and try to comfort her, her tiny hands would claw at my clothing, completely unaware of me or her surroundings. It would take a few minutes to calm her down during these episodes.

Child psychologists acknowledge that by ten months old, children recognize their parents' faces, their voices, and their scent among other cues, causing the child to "attach" to his or her parents. So although Laurel doesn't have distinct memories of her dad, she had already attached to him, and seemed to sense the absence of the voice she no longer heard and the face she no longer saw. A few weeks before September 11, she had started kissing pictures of "Dada" when he wasn't home. Months later she was still kissing her daddy's picture.

Laurel was three years old when she started seeing a child play therapist. The therapist explained that children use play to communicate at an early age, because they do not know the words or even have an understanding of their emotions. Laurel was experiencing severe mood swings. She would become angry for no apparent reason, yelling and screaming, completely out of control. A few minutes later she would calm down on her own and be very apologetic, hugging me and telling me she loved me. A little while later she could become angry again, sometimes cycling through these outbursts multiple times a day. She also had developed a fear of men, which I had inadvertently perpetuated. There were only a few men in her life, and none were those she saw on an everyday basis.

When Laurel asked questions about her dad, I explained to her that daddy had been flying the airplane and there had been some bad men who had made the airplane crash into the ground. After Laurel began her therapy sessions, the therapist discovered that I had unintentionally given Laurel the idea that all men were bad by calling the hijackers "bad men." Once I realized what I had done, I explained to my daughter that anyone could do bad things, even "ladies," which was how Laurel referred to all females. Within months she was less angry and the mood swings decreased.

Once Laurel was old enough to ask these types of questions, I wasn't always sure how to answer them. Her therapist assured me that children usually ask questions when they are ready for the answers. She helped me figure out ways to answer Laurel's questions in a way she would understand. Initially, I was concerned that if I said too much about the plane crashing, Laurel would be afraid to fly. Her therapist explained that children her age do not develop the fear of flying the way an adult might.

It was a challenge. Sometimes Laurel would ask the same question over the course of a few days, weeks, or months. Each time Laurel asked, I answered her question as simply as possible, telling her that the bad people on the plane had also died, and her daddy had helped save the lives of people on the ground. I omitted the more disturbing details.

Through play therapy, we learned that Laurel was afraid something would happen to me if I had to travel. I had traveled for work in the past, but after I left my position with Ortho Biotech in 2003, I only traveled occasionally. Knowing that she was uncomfortable when I traveled, I called often and tried to not be gone for more than seventy-two hours. It didn't make a difference whether I was driving, taking a train, or flying on a plane; Laurel was just afraid something would happen to me. Her therapist explained that this was a normal fear for a child her age to have, especially one who has already lost a parent. As she has grown older, she is less fearful when I leave but knows she can call me whenever she needs to and I will answer.

When Laurel started preschool, her teacher expressed concern about Laurel's ability to pay attention in the classroom. What Laurel's teacher described and her therapist confirmed was a state of hypervigilance; Laurel was in a constant "red alert," a symptom observed in someone who has experienced a trauma. Laurel was looking around, observing, and listening to the conversations around her, unconsciously anticipating something unexpected and bad to happen. At this point, Laurel's therapy shifted to dealing with the anger attributed to losing her dad, lessening her fear of men, and helping her feel safe so she would be able to improve her focus at school.

Laurel frequently asked to see the photo album of her baby pictures. There were lots of pictures of her and LeRoy. After looking at the album, she would be inconsolable, crying uncontrollably and begging for her daddy to come back. Maybe a month would go by before she asked to see the pictures again. I started making excuses. I wasn't sure where the album was, or we didn't have time because we were on our way out. I knew she wanted to see the pictures, but it was too upsetting for both of us.

Laurel liked me to tell her Daddy Stories. I would tell her about the silly things her dad did to make me laugh, and stories he had told me from when he was a little boy. Her favorite stories were the ones that involved just her and LeRoy: how daddy was the one who noticed her first tooth coming in when they had been out to lunch together; how her dad had taken her in his arms and danced with her, announcing he was practicing for their father/daughter dance at her wedding.

One day I will have to answer the more difficult questions. One day Laurel will ask me where he's buried. She will probably Google his name, and hear her father's voice on the Air Traffic Control tapes as he tried to fight off the hijackers. But for now, I encourage the pride Laurel feels in LeRoy, knowing that her daddy saved lives. I've shown her the thank-you letters and cards we have received from people who either were in the Washington, D.C. area or who had children there on September 11, 2001. She sees all the awards I have received on her dad's behalf. I even let her take the Congressional Gold Medal to school for show and tell in the third grade. And she knows there is a plaque in the U.S. Capitol with her dad's name on it in tribute to the passengers and crew of Flight 93.

15

CHANGES

"In the situation room
There was a toy world
And a flight costume
And a picture of—
A refinery plume.
And there were war profiteers giving three cheers.
A nation great
A Church and a State
A pair of towers
And a balance of powers.
A Grand Old Party to war in a rush
And a quiet Dick Cheney whispering, "Hush.". . . .
Goodnight jets flying over the plume . . . .
Goodnight towers.
And goodnight balance of powers."

—Erich Origen and Gan Golan, *Goodnight Bush*

L eRoy and I had begun house hunting in August
2001. Knowing we planned to have more children,
we were looking at larger homes located farther north
from where we lived. I wanted him to be closer to the

airport, so his commute would be shorter, allowing us more family time. Immediately following September 11, I decided to stay in the Marlton area. Marlton had good school districts, and I felt comfortable there. I knew where to take my dry cleaning, which stores were the best for groceries, and I had extremely supportive neighbors.

Back in the summer of 2001, LeRoy and I had made a list of things we wanted in a house. We loved our porch, and LeRoy liked having the house backed up to woods because of the privacy. We wanted a house on an acre or two of land. We both loved wood-burning fireplaces and gourmet kitchens. I had always wanted a window seat; LeRoy wanted a six-burner gas stove. Even though we wanted a basement, LeRoy hated how low the ceilings usually were and how little sunlight would filter in.

Several months after September 11, I went ahead with the home search that LeRoy and I had begun. When I drove into one of the new home developments about a month into my search, I found a floor plan with everything we had included on our list. My new home would sit on about an acre and a half of land. The floor plan showed a gourmet kitchen, and the family room had a large window under which the builder was able to add a window seat. A wood-burning fireplace in the family room would get a lot of use during the winter.

The basement had an extra high ceiling and a walkout that provided natural light. We would have four bedrooms—one for myself, one for Laurel, and one for my son, Alden, whose arrival was eagerly anticipated. The extra room would be for my parents who visited frequently to give me a helping hand. I had an office on the main floor where I could prepare my presentations to hospital staff or cancer support groups.

I moved into my new home on March 21, 2003, the day before the war in Iraq began. My parents, along with my brother and his wife, drove down from Canada to help with the move. This should have been a happy occasion. But I was preoccupied by thoughts of the war, even with the televisions packed away. I wanted to avoid the inevitable—hearing the first war casualties.

LeRoy's friend Steve had also served as a pilot in the U.S. Air Force, and I wanted him to help me understand the impending war the United States was planning to wage on Iraq. I avoided watching the news as much as I could, since there were still many news stories that would end with footage of Flight 175 crashing into the South Tower of the World Trade Center or a shot of the Shanksville crash site. I thought that maybe in my avoidance of the mainstream media, I had missed important information on why the United States was going to war. I had heard about the weapons of mass destruction. But it seemed strange that other NATO countries, including my own country, Canada, were not convinced that Iraq posed any significant threat when presented with the same information. At the very least, there had to be proof of links between Iraq and al-Qaeda. But Steve confirmed what I was afraid of: I hadn't missed anything at all.

As the years had passed, my distrust for the Bush administration had only gotten worse. That President Bush remained in that Florida classroom minutes after he was informed about the attack is incomprehensible.

There was one thing Steve said that I never will forget. He said, "People are going to die." Those words would echo in my brain for years. I didn't want more people to die. Worse still was the implicit understanding that the war was being fought for the people who had died on September 11. If that was the reason men and women were risking their lives, I wish those of us who had lost loved ones could have had a voice. If anyone had told me they were fighting the war in Iraq for LeRoy, I would have begged them not to.

I understood why the U.S. government had gone into Afghanistan. This was al-Qaeda's base of operations. They had trained their terrorists and formulated plots to destroy the United States and its allies. The American people, feeling vulnerable in the post-September 11 world, were manipulated into thinking the war was a form of justice. However, I couldn't understand why the United States was invading Iraq. One of the first and most disturbing stories I heard on the news was about an American Muslim Army sergeant who had launched a grenade-and-rifle attack against his fellow soldiers. Hasan Akbar had thrown grenades into troop tents at Camp Pennsylvania in Kuwait on a March morning and then fired on soldiers in the ensuing chaos. Two officers were killed and fourteen others injured in the attack. Prosecutors later said during his trial that the attack was driven by Akbar's religious extremism. This was just three days after the war had started.

I heard the audio coming from the television, and as I tried to process the information, I remember becoming immediately upset and agitated and then more anxious as the hours went by. My chest was tight and I was having difficulty breathing. Later that day, I was driving my parents out for dinner to celebrate my mom's birthday and I started to feel lightheaded. I didn't say anything because I didn't want to ruin my mom's evening. My family had all pitched in to help me get moved into my new home, and I wanted them to have a nice relaxing meal, without having to worry about me.

When we got to the restaurant, I excused myself

and called my therapist, who explained that those first fatalities had triggered my PTSD. After months of disassociating, I thought I had perfected my ability to numb myself to pain, especially when I wasn't directly affected. But these first stories of the lives lost in Iraq affected me in a profound way. I could imagine the families of the soldiers who were dying. Their deaths seemed worse than those on September 11, perhaps because the Iraq war was based on a lie, a lie about Iraq possessing weapons of mass destruction. The war had opened up fresh pain that I was unable to numb. In my mind I linked the deaths in Iraq to the deaths on September 11. If September 11 hadn't happened, there wouldn't have been a war in Iraq. I felt beaten, and any progress I had made in dealing with LeRoy's death had been undone.

On May 1, 2003, less than two months after the war started, President George W. Bush announced that the Iraq war was over. "Mission accomplished," he said while aboard the USS Abraham Lincoln, wearing a flight suit. LeRoy had worked his entire life for the privilege of wearing a flight suit. Starting with an after-school job cleaning a doctor's office to be able to pay for flight lessons, to being accepted into the U.S. Air Force Academy, to his seven years of active duty in the U.S. Air Force, LeRoy had worked hard, earning the rank of major and the privilege to wear the uniform of his profession. There would be many days when, as much as I tried to be positive and strong, something would derail my best intentions. Seeing the president dressed in a flight suit was by far one of the most personal and painful acts of disrespect that I had witnessed. The day's events would be chronicled as one of the biggest missteps in the president's time in office, even by his own admission. And, as we soon discovered, the war was far from over.

Therapy sessions, my last months of work, and our new home consumed our spring and summer. As September drew closer, the phone calls escalated with requests for interviews or my attendance at a memorial event. This second anniversary was no easier than the first. I could feel myself sinking deeper into grief that would start in August—LeRoy and I both had August birthdays, and we had celebrated our birthdays together for six years. Now I refused to celebrate my birthday at all. No gifts, no cards, no cake, no saying "Happy Birthday" because it wasn't happy.

Ellen Saracini, who also now dreaded birthdays, told me one year her friends had given her a cake that said "Birthday Ellen," purposely leaving off the word "Happy." I liked that story, because at least it showed that her friends understood how the occasion made her feel. Once the birthdays were over, it would only be a few days before another anniversary of September 11.

There had been one unexpected bright spot that fall. In September 2003, the Department of Defense was launching a Titan IVB rocket from Cape Canaveral in Florida. The launch would be dedicated to Major LeRoy W. Homer, Jr. since LeRoy had served in the Air Force, and the entire family had been invited to witness the launch as guests of the Air Force Space Command and the 45th Space Wing. We were invited to sit in on the mission briefing with Team Titan, where we were presented with commemorative coins and the mission's official flight suit patch. The patch was decorated with stars and stripes and depicted a rocket and a B-36 bomber. Above the phrase *Vos Intuebor*, meaning "I'll be watching you," was our last name, Homer.

The launch was scheduled for midnight, so when it was almost time, my parents, my siblings, and LeRoy's mother and sisters and their families were taken onto the roof of a base building where we could get a clear view of the launch pad. As we heard the countdown start over a loudspeaker, we counted along until the moment of liftoff. The night sky lit up so brightly, it looked like daytime for a few brief seconds, and then it was gone. We could still see the rocket through the scattered clouds as it made its rapid ascent into the atmosphere. I felt the awe and the thrill of being able to witness something so amazing. And then almost immediately, I felt sadness. LeRoy was not there to see it with me. LeRoy, who had once considered becoming an astronaut, would have been beyond thrilled to witness a launch.

I returned from Florida on September 10. The media coverage, constant and unavoidable, intensified my despair. An anniversary of someone's death is strange in many ways. I felt overwhelmed by the many phone calls from people who wanted me to know they were thinking of me that day. Did they not realize I thought about LeRoy every single day of the year?

16

LOST RELATIONSHIPS

*"The ultimate measure of a man is not where he stands
in moments of comfort and convenience, but where he stands at times
of challenge and controversy."*

—Martin Luther King, Jr.

The second anniversary had passed but as the weather began to change and the days were becoming shorter, my loneliness worsened. I was still getting to know my neighbors, and had begun to feel alienated by our group of friends, especially when I learned through a Christmas letter that someone was expecting. I called this person crying, trying to understand how someone who I had spoken with on a regular basis, who had been in our wedding party, would not have taken the time to call and tell me this news directly.

I had once read in a booklet on coping with the loss

of a spouse: "Some of your married friends will drift away in time, because you have less in common with them than before. This is a normal process and you should not take it personally when it occurs." But I was hysterical. Why would someone write something so horrible? I had just lost my husband. Now, apparently, I was going to lose my friends, too, and I shouldn't be upset about it? I had the phone number of a crisis counselor and, still hysterical, told him what I had just read. As he tried to calm me, he explained that most of what I would read about grieving was geared to older widows. He asked me if I had lost any friends. I hadn't. But that had been only a few weeks after LeRoy died.

Now here it was two years later, and it seemed the book had been right after all. Looking back, I remember being at a barbecue with some of LeRoy's friends on Labor Day weekend, 2001. Most of them were guys he had flown with while he was stationed at McGuire. Many of these same guys had been hired by United Airlines, and all lived within an hour of each other. As some of the guys had married, the friendship circle had expanded to include wives and babies. And I remember thinking, *If something ever happened to LeRoy, would these people still be my friends?* I wasn't thinking about a plane crash. I worried more about him driving home from Kennedy Airport after flying all night. A couple of the guys were in our wedding. We had even vacationed together. These people were an important part of LeRoy's life; knowing this, I had made them important in my life, too.

In a bizarre coincidence, one of LeRoy's friends and a fellow United Airlines pilot had bid for the same schedule as LeRoy had for the month of September 2001. At his barbecue that weekend, this friend jokingly blamed LeRoy for taking his line that month. Everyone preferred the Newark departures because the airport was closer to home than JFK or LaGuardia. But LeRoy's seniority had "awarded" him the schedule that included flying Flight 93 on September 11, 2001.

Had the situation been reversed, I know without a doubt LeRoy would have made sure he was present in the life of his friends' families, especially under such horrendous circumstances. Even if it was uncomfortable, even if it was painful, he would have been there. I'm not sure anyone can fully understand where an individual's compassion and empathy come from. But I know some people have these qualities and some people don't, and you won't know who has what until the friend you thought would be there isn't. The loss of our friends was something I discussed at length with my therapist. Her perspective was that certain people were not capable of giving me the emotional support I needed.

Whenever I felt abandoned by these former friends,

I would recite this mantra to myself: "It's not their fault. They're not capable of giving me emotional support. They can't help it." But over time, I came up with my own perception. There are certain expectations we have of others that most people would say are reasonable. One of these is one's work ethic. An employer expects an employee to have a good work ethic. Most people would agree a poor work ethic is not acceptable in the work place. So in this same vein, I believe that how you treat people, especially the people closest to you, should not be debatable. If the person is someone you truly value, you don't desert him or her. You figure out a way to be there.

Given that most of my husband's friends were guys he had served with in the military—where forming complex relationships through life and death are part and parcel—I held them to an even higher standard. When I mentioned my disappointment that Laurel didn't have her dad's friends around to tell her their own stories about him, my therapist suggested that perhaps LeRoy's friends assumed I was moving on with my life and had other friendships. So I reached out to them, letting them know we hoped they would be a part of our lives. Even so, these relationships have dissolved into an annual Christmas card exchange.

* * *

I hosted Christmas for the first time in my new home in December 2003. My family had skipped Christmas the year before since the 2001 holidays had proved so difficult. I wasn't looking forward to the holidays anymore than I had for the past two years, but Laurel was now three years old. She deserved to have Christmas memories. I took Laurel to the Christmas tree farm where we had always picked out our tree. LeRoy loved Christmas, and Christmas traditions. We always took a picture in front of the tree before we had it cut down and tied to the roof of our car. I made sure Laurel and I had our picture taken in front of the tree we bought that year. I made the same Christmas cookies I had made every year, and Laurel helped with the decorating. I bought gifts, decorated the tree and the house, and took Laurel to see Santa at the mall.

I even put up a few Christmas lights outside, which I had never done before. I was getting frustrated because I couldn't figure out the best way to string the lights so that we'd have enough electrical outlets; before long, I started to cry. I cried because I was angry. Putting up the lights had been LeRoy's job, not mine. I knew I really wasn't mad at him; I was mad at the situation. Laurel deserved to have the Christmas she would have had if LeRoy were here.

That year, my sister found a woman who made

beautiful personalized Christmas stockings. Heather asked me if it was okay to have her make a stocking for LeRoy, too, but there was no question. Every year, regardless of who hosts Christmas, LeRoy's stocking hangs alongside everyone else's. He will always be a part of our family's Christmas traditions.

17

THE JUSTICE DEPARTMENT

"The truth will set you free."

—John 8:32

S andy and I had requested a meeting with the Justice Department to hear all radio communications surrounding Flight 93, from the gate at Newark until the plane went down in Shanksville. We were granted this meeting in January 2004. This information, along with what we had heard on the cockpit voice recorder, the ACRS transmissions for Flight 93, and the information from the flight data recorder, helped us fill the gaps in our understanding of what had occurred in the cockpit that morning.

What we knew: Jason was piloting the plane on the morning of September 11; LeRoy was making the radio calls. I had heard LeRoy on the radio many times before when I would fly with him on his work trips.

United Airlines has a channel broadcasting the transmissions between the cockpit and Air Traffic Control on their in-flight entertainment system. When Sandy and I traveled to the Department of Justice office in Alexandria, Virginia, we were able to listen to all of LeRoy and Jason's radio transmissions from the moment he pushed back from Gate 17 at Newark International Airport to the end. Since Jason was flying that leg, most of the air traffic control radio calls were LeRoy's. I wasn't sure what I would learn but I wanted to understand the morning's events as best I could, and both Sandy and I thought having all the information presented together would help.

Every minute I heard LeRoy talking brought him closer to the moment when I would never hear his voice again. I felt like I needed to warn him of the danger ahead. But I couldn't warn him because the worst had already happened. The transcript showed the cockpit receiving the message I had sent to LeRoy making sure he was okay. Then the message from Ed Ballinger, the United Dispatcher on duty, was sent, alerting Jason and LeRoy: "Beware any cockpit intrusions—two a/c [aircraft] hit the World Trade Center." Two minutes later, Jason Dahl responded, "Ed, confirm latest mssg, plz." Once the cockpit was breached, the autopilot, which could be described as the airplane version of cruise control, was turned off, but it was then turned on again one minute later. From what I had learned from LeRoy, pilots typically switch to autopilot once they reach their cruising altitude.

The hijackers were manually flying the airplane with the autopilot on. This didn't seem intentional, especially when one of the hijackers said, "Inform them, and tell them to talk to the pilot. Bring the pilot back." They were having problems flying the plane, a plane that had been operating fine just minutes before. Something had been done in the cockpit to make the airplane more difficult to fly. This may have given the flight attendants and passengers enough time to organize themselves and disrupt the hijacking. Realizing they would not be able to reach their target, the hijackers made the decision to crash the plane. Both LeRoy and Jason played an integral part in the plane not reaching its target.

A few months after my visit to the Justice Department, my claim with the Victim Compensation Fund was settled. Meeting with my lawyer and going through all the steps to put the claim together had taken much longer than I had expected. I was glad it was over. Discussing the value of LeRoy's life was a topic that reduced me to tears. I had hoped once the claim was settled, I would feel a sense of relief. But the emotional roller coaster of my life was far from over.

I had left my job a month earlier, but was still busy

planning for our second fundraiser for the LeRoy W. Homer, Jr. Foundation. Our first fundraiser in August 2002 was a huge success. It hadn't yet been a year since the attacks, and sympathy still ran high for September 11 causes. We had a lot of wonderful volunteers who helped us with our fundraising events, and with the media attention surrounding the anniversary, we were able to raise a good amount of money. We awarded our first scholarships in the spring of 2003 and have continued to select scholarship recipients each spring in the years since. In the spring of 2004, we were working on our next fundraiser. It was a lot of work, but it was also a great distraction and it felt good to do something so positive in LeRoy's honor.

By this point, the 2004 presidential election campaign was underway. I tried hard to avoid getting too caught up in the campaign rhetoric. I didn't watch the debates and changed channels if there was any footage of the president making a speech. I couldn't imagine Bush being re-elected. During the 9/11 Commission's investigation, it was determined that the president had been briefed on August 6, 2001, that "a group of [Osama] bin Laden supporters were planning attacks in the United States with explosives." In December 2004, 9/11 Commission Chairman Tom Kean gave his assessment that the 9/11 attacks could have been prevented.

The Iraq war had not ended as the president had declared a year earlier. The soldiers who made it home came back with physical or emotional wounds, sometimes both. At the time, no one spoke about the individuals who served their country and came home alive, only to commit suicide. The innocent civilians of Iraq—men, women, and children—were rarely mentioned in news reports.

I had tried to watch the hearings when Condoleezza Rice testified for the 9/11 Commission in May 2004. All I saw and heard was someone who seemed prepped, who knew how to side-step difficult questions. After listening for only a few minutes and hearing her say more than once during her testimony that "there was no silver bullet that could have prevented the 9/11 attacks," I decided not to watch anymore. I was hoping someone would apologize. It's easier to forgive someone who is sorry for the hurt they have caused. But that wasn't going to happen, and it didn't seem like any real information would be forthcoming.

Before the information from the Commission became public, the Department of Justice held a meeting for the family members of both crew and passengers. They wanted to provide us with all the information they had gathered prior to the report's publication and subsequent release to the media. Ellen and I attended the meeting together in June 2004 in

Princeton, New Jersey. There were probably a hundred or so people at this meeting, which included family members from all four flights. All the audio the government had obtained from September 11 was played, and the phone call transcripts read. This included calls from the other flights, which I had been unaware of and had not yet heard.

A few weeks later, on a day that had otherwise started out okay, I received a package. It was a copy of *The 9/11 Commission Report*, with a card that read, "Please accept this complimentary copy from the publisher."

18

DEALING WITH PTSD

"The lowest ebb is the turn of the tide."

—Henry Wadsworth Longfellow, "Loss and Gain"

In October 2004, President Bush made a campaign stop in Marlton, New Jersey to give a speech on "A Safer America" about two hundred yards from the memorial garden built to honor LeRoy; I was not invited. Invitations to the White House had been extended to me and my family, both before and after the president's Marlton campaign stop, but for some reason I hadn't been invited to this event. It didn't really matter. I would have declined the invitation, just as I had declined the invitations to the White House.

Instead, I chose to be interviewed by the local South Jersey *Courier-Post* at LeRoy's memorial and to discuss some of my concerns about the president's decisions over the past four years, from his inability in preventing the September 2001 attacks to my feelings about the Iraq war. I wasn't an American citizen, so I couldn't vote. This was the one thing I could do. However, it was only one local newspaper interview and ultimately, it didn't make a difference. In November 2004, the American people re-elected President Bush.

In May 2005, United Airlines, which had been operating in Chapter 11 bankruptcy since 2002, defaulted on their employee pension plan in order to cut costs. When I had applied for the Victim Compensation Fund in 2002, the process involved first determining how much LeRoy's life would have been worth if he had lived out his life. Then "collateral offsets" were deducted from whatever award I would receive. This decision was made by Kenneth Feinberg, the special master of the fund. Collateral offsets included life insurance and future pension payments. Despite the likelihood that United Airlines, already in bankruptcy, would default on its pension plan, this possibility was repeatedly dismissed by Kenneth Feinberg and the administrators of the Compensation Fund, and future pension payments were deducted from the compensation I was awarded.

When United did ultimately default, the Victim Compensation Fund was nullified, and the pension plan for United pilot retirees—a group Ellen, Sandy, Miriam, and I had become a part of when our husbands had died—was taken over by a government agency, the Pension Benefit Guaranty Corporation, who would determine the monthly pensions. I lost over 40 percent of LeRoy's pension when the PBGC took over the pension plan. I didn't realize this until December of 2010 when I received my final determination letter stating that for six years the PBGC had been reviewing my case, as well as the cases of the other United Airlines retirees. When the final determination was made, I calculated that between losing a portion of my pension in the United bankruptcy, the initial default by United to the PBGC, and now the final determination, I would now receive 28 percent of the pension amount I had received in the months after September 2001. As a result, Ellen, Sandy, Miriam, and I have joined a lawsuit with other United employee retirees who are in the same situation, hoping to recoup our continued financial losses.

* * *

It had been more than five years since LeRoy died, yet the pain was still constant. My friends mentioned how much better I seemed, but I wasn't better. I had only gained back some of the weight I had lost and had learned how to pretend, to put on the mask that made it seem like I was holding things together. It was important to me that my children felt secure. I wanted them to have the best childhood possible. I didn't want them to ever have to worry about me, so I put on my happy face and forced myself up and out of the house. I was physically present, and emotionally absent.

I had done everything I thought would help me get better. I had been taking medication and had spent two years in therapy. But I still was far away from enjoying my life in any meaningful way. There were moments in the day when the kids said or did something that would make me feel genuine pleasure. But they were only moments. And then I would wonder, as I often did, how I had managed to survive like this for so long.

I was inundated with reminders of an event that had affected the whole world. I remember watching the movie, *Love Actually,* one night, thinking a romantic comedy would be a good distraction. As I listened to the voiceover at the very beginning of the movie, I heard, "When the planes hit the Twin Towers. . . none of the phone calls from people on board were messages of hate or revenge—they were all messages of love." It was one of those moments when I knew that instead of love, I would always be surrounded by references to September 11.

Sometimes I wouldn't realize until it was too late that I had put myself in a situation for which I was unprepared. In the spring of 2002, I went to my annual OB/GYN appointment. I had made the appointment after I received the reminder postcard in the mail. But it wasn't until I was making my way into the building, a building full of pregnant women, that I realized what I had done. I hadn't expected to sit in the waiting area reflecting on how I would probably never be pregnant again. By the time my doctor was ready to examine me, I was a mess. I cried during my appointment and in my car on the ride home.

One morning as I was driving Laurel to preschool, I noticed a plane flying overhead. Our house sits beneath the flight path of planes waiting to land at the Philadelphia Airport, and Laurel and I loved watching the planes circle over our house from the hammock in the backyard. Together we would lie back and try to figure out if we could determine the airlines based on the plane's colors.

But the plane I saw on this particular day was different. It was a much smaller plane, and it was flying at a low altitude. As I drove up to Laurel's preschool, I noticed the plane circling the area, flying farther out and then coming back and circling over the school. I could feel the fear creeping into my chest. I didn't understand what I was seeing. Trying to sound calm, I told Laurel we needed to leave. I had already undone her car-seat straps. Laurel reminded me she wasn't strapped in, but I told her she didn't need her car seat right now and she could just sit back in the seat like a big girl. As I made a sharp turn to get out of the drop-off area and away from her school, Laurel slid across the back seat. I drove far enough away so the plane was no longer circling above us, and then I turned into a store parking lot.

I called 411 and got the number for the police station. When a female dispatcher answered the phone, I tried to explain to her, in as calm a voice as I could manage, what I had seen. The dispatcher put me on hold for a couple minutes, then came back on the line and told me the area I had described was being sprayed for mosquitoes; there was nothing to worry about. I thanked her for the information, and ended the call. With my head on the steering wheel, I cried out all the tension.

Laurel may have asked me what was wrong, but I'm not sure what I said. I pulled myself together, then got out of the car, strapped Laurel back in her car seat, and drove her back to school. Having first been diagnosed with PTSD in 2001, this was my first triggered episode. Seeing the plane hovering so close had made me experience the intensity of the emotions I felt the day LeRoy's plane had crashed into the ground. Although I had tried through the years to avoid situations that I knew would trigger traumatic stress, there would always be these unavoidable instances in which I would feel like time had taken me back to the day that had destroyed everything.

When *United 93* was selected to be screened at the Tribeca Film Festival, I decided to attend. I didn't want to hear about it second hand, as I had with the television productions. And I didn't want to be afraid of a movie, which I knew through no fault of the film's creators was not going to be an accurate portrayal of events because of the continuing misrepresentation of the CVR. But the little details included in the film—the casual conversation between the pilots as they make their way to the plane, LeRoy talking about having a baby at home, the hot sauce in the flight bag, the things I knew were true—were the parts of the movie that took me back to my darkest days.

In 2006 I started to research PTSD on my own. After two years of cognitive behavioral therapy and grief counseling, I knew I still was dealing with the post-traumatic stress. Perhaps if I could deal with that, I would be able to feel something close to normal. I read entire books discussing the different treatment methods. I decided that the one thing, the only thing, I could do was try the various treatment methods until something worked.

The treatment that seemed to hold the most promise was eye movement desensitization and reprocessing. I had read that EMDR worked on the theory that when a person suffers a trauma, the brain is not able to process the information like it normally would. So instead of being filed away in the parts of your brain where memory is stored, the memory of the trauma stays right in the forefront of your mind, always present. EMDR helps the brain process the trauma so that although you still remember what has happened, the feelings associated with the event are not as intense. Unlike traditional therapy, EMDR works within about three sessions per traumatic event—if it works at all. Since I had suffered an initial trauma, with subsequent stressful periods over the years, I could expect therapy to take several months. The closest EMDR therapist was in Delaware, about an hour away from my home.

I started EMDR in January 2007. I met with Meryl, my therapist, several times before I started therapy. She wanted to make sure I would have the coping skills to deal with the feelings and emotions that would surface during the course of an hour of therapy. Meryl asked me to envision a place, either real or imagined, where I felt peaceful and safe. I had to picture everything about this place in my mind and then describe it to her. I imagined a wooden deck on the back of a house. I was always sitting in a chair on the left side of this deck with my feet pulled up underneath me. I was wearing a cable-knit sweater because it was early evening and there was a slight breeze in the air. I could hear the sea's gentle waves, while occasionally in the background birds sang. Meryl needed to understand the history of my PTSD, beginning with the initial trauma and continuing with the events that had transpired since. If I ever felt I was headed towards an emotional breaking point, she would redirect me to this place I had created in my mind.

We made a list of specific events and situations. One memory that was particularly hard for me was my first phone call to the United Airlines flight office on September 11. I couldn't even talk about it without my voice choking, as I experienced the hurt and betrayal I felt towards the woman who had assured me, "Everything is okay." After a single session of EMDR, which involved talking through the incident while using hand-held pulsers that rhythmically tapped in one hand and then the other, I was able to work through my feelings. All the anger and hurt I had carried around for years surrounding this incident were gone. I no longer experienced an emotional reaction towards this moment and now rarely think about it.

Meryl and I made our way through each issue individually: my feelings towards United Airlines, my sense of abandonment at the loss of our friends, and my frustration with the media for ignoring LeRoy's role on Flight 93, among others. After five months of weekly sessions, I had turned a corner. For the first time in six years, I felt a glimmer of hope.

19

ELECTION NIGHT 2008

"Change has come to America."

—Barack Obama, Presidential Acceptance Speech,

November 4, 2008

I was in Florida on Tuesday, November 4, 2008, on a trip with my kids to Disney World. I had decided to wear my "Bush's Last Day" T-shirt on Election Day, unsure of what kind of reaction the sentiment would elicit in the state that had been involved in the controversial vote recount in the 2000 presidential election. The first thing I noticed was how many people were wearing Barack Obama T-shirts. Even the Disney employees complimented me on my shirt. One man went so far as to say, "You know, Florida cheated in 2000." I had tried to avoid the coverage of the campaign as much as I could. I didn't like how the candidates disparaged each other, how every single comment made by a candidate was analyzed, their families evaluated. It was a nasty race.

My first real recollection (and positive impression) of Barack Obama occurred during his campaign in October 2008 when during a debate with Senator Clinton he said: "I was friends with Hillary Clinton before we started this campaign; I will be friends with Hillary Clinton after this campaign is over." It was refreshing to see a politician who had something positive to say about his opponent.

After that, I started to pay more attention to this man who seemed to be level-headed and capable of doing the job he was seeking. When Senator McCain announced that Sarah Palin was his running mate choice, I began exploring other options, just in case they were elected. Both of my children are dual citizens; American citizens by birth, and Canadian citizens because of my own citizenship. I wasn't going to live in the United States for another four years under a president who would continue to fight a senseless war, and a vice president whose major appeal seemed to be her appearance. I didn't want my children growing up in an environment of apathy to the countless lives lost in the past eight years. But as the election neared, I allowed myself a small amount of optimism. Barack Obama could win.

I had always disliked change. But this was a change

I needed, a change my children needed, a change the country needed. I've always believed you don't have a right to complain about the way things are if you're not willing to do something to pitch in. I didn't have a vote, but I could donate my time. In October, I called the local Democratic National Committee. In the weeks before the election, I worked for the Obama campaign making phone calls to people in the battleground state of Pennsylvania. I felt empowered. I made calls right up until I left for Florida a few days before the election. The general reaction from the people I called was overwhelmingly positive.

Eight years earlier, on Election Night 2000, I had gone to bed after Al Gore was declared the president-elect only to wake up to the crushing turn of events. This time I would stay up as long as it took to learn the true election results.

My kids were sleeping, the lights were off, and I watched CNN with no sound. This reminded me of those first months after September 11 when I was unable to sleep and would read the crawling text at the bottom of the screen. As I watched the votes coming in, I couldn't help but wonder what the impetus would be behind America's decision. Would it be the fear of terrorism, the downward spiral of the economy, the wars in Iraq and Afghanistan? Then all of a sudden, the results were in. It was all over. We had a new president-elect.

Before I could celebrate, I needed to hear the speeches that would make it official. I listened to what John McCain said, and I sensed his loyalty and dedication to serving his country—something that hadn't come across, in my opinion, during his campaign. Then I waited to hear President-Elect Obama speak.

Before he stepped up to the podium at Grant Park, I noticed the flags that adorned the stage. The American flag had never really been part of my consciousness, as I didn't grow up in the United States. When the flag was handed to me at LeRoy's memorial service, it became the thing I did not want to claim. One of the U.S. Air Force pilots LeRoy had worked with had told me once that it didn't matter what it was—"If you wrapped the American flag around it, Americans would buy it." I had heard political commentators describe this as "patriotism by fear."

Up till then, the flag for me had represented all the government's lies: the deception about weapons of mass destruction; the justification for their delayed response to Hurricane Katrina; their rationalization for the use of torture; and, of course, a refusal to admit that acting on warnings of a terrorist attack involving commercial aircraft might have saved thousands of lives.

But as I looked at the flag that night, I didn't feel the usual turmoil. It looked the same, but I didn't feel the same. It was no longer a symbol of the eight years that had passed. The flag had changed in a split second, and I now felt optimistic.

EPILOGUE

"Memory can tell us only what we were,
In company with those we loved."

—Richard Fife, "Memory Can Tell Us Only What We Were"

If not for the individuals on United Flight 93, the loss of life within the legislative branch of government would have turned this country into chaos far beyond what we experienced in the aftermath of September 11.

I went to the U.S. Capitol for the first time in March 2007; LeRoy had posthumously been inducted into the ranks of the Tuskegee Airmen because of his actions on Flight 93, and when the Tuskegee Airmen received the Congressional Gold Medal, I was invited to attend on LeRoy's behalf. Two days before the eighth anniversary of September 11, the family members of the passengers and crew were invited to the unveiling of a bronze plaque which has the names of all forty individuals who died on that flight. The plaque reads in part: "Their sacrifice not only saved countless lives, but may have saved the U.S. Capitol from destruction." Since then I have been invited to the U.S. Capitol for other events, and as I walk through various areas of this beautiful building, I experience an immense feeling of pride. My husband was instrumental in the fact that this building still stands.

For awhile, everyone wore pins and had bumper stickers on their cars that said "United We Stand" and "We Will Never Forget." But in the years that have passed, most people avoid thinking about that day. In the days that followed the attacks, there was a sense that we needed to unite against the threat to our country to make sure nothing like this happened again. It was a noble goal, yet this sentiment feels like it has been boiled down to one day a year. It was important for the country to move forward from that terrible day, but at times it feels like only a small number of people who were deeply affected by the attack still care enough to continue their efforts, such as the work that has been ongoing to complete the Flight 93 memorial.

I've learned over time that most people will never fully understand the enormity of what happened to me. The expression "If someone could walk in your shoes" is, after all, just an expression. We all feel, think, and live in different ways. We each experience the relationships in our lives differently, which makes it difficult for others, even my closest friends, to fully identify with me, even if they experience similar circumstances. I'm hoping that sharing my experiences over these past few years will help others who have suffered loss to know that someone understands.

I feel very fortunate for the people who did step into my life at a time when I needed help the most. Digna, who was my neighbor and Laurel's babysitter on September 11, 2001, remains one of my dearest friends. There were other neighbors, friends from church, and a couple of coworkers—people who I didn't know very well before September 11, who are always there to give me a helping hand when I need it.

Many people are identified by their profession, nationality, or appearance; I am identified as a September 11 widow, first and foremost, and certainly not by choice. It is difficult to meet new people without the subject being mentioned. Even if I say my husband passed away, most will ask how he died, thus starting a conversation that will form first impressions. I can see the look of pity and also the desire to get away from me as soon as possible, as if I have an affliction that is contagious. On multiple occasions, I have heard one person explaining to someone else who I am: "That's the widow of the pilot that crashed on September 11 in Pennsylvania." These people are evidently not concerned with me overhearing, making me want to get away from the situation as quickly as possible to avoid being made the center of attention. I think I should be the one to decide if and when someone should have personal information about me. But some people enjoy being the one to tell the story. It must make them feel important. I don't enjoy the attention or the pity my situation evokes. The end result is I have a difficult time trusting peoples' intentions.

I'm not sure how many September 11 memorials will be built when all is said and done. Schools, streets, and post offices have been renamed in memory of all who had died. In 2008, the new operations building bearing LeRoy's name was dedicated at Wright-Patterson Air Force Base in Dayton, Ohio. The first part of the Flight 93 memorial will be dedicated on September 10, 2011.

I started back to work as a nursing instructor for a local community college in 2007. I enjoy my career and being able to work part time allows me to devote time to The LeRoy W. Homer, Jr. Foundation. The Foundation is still unfamiliar to many, but we continue to thrive; as long as we are carrying out our mission, I am proud of what our board members, volunteers, and contributors accomplish.

To date, our scholarship recipients have made us proud. All have gone on to four-year colleges, several at Embry-Riddle Aeronautical University, a premier university offering aviation-related degrees. Past scholarship recipients have also attended the U.S. Naval Academy in Annapolis, Maryland, and the U.S. Air Force Academy in Colorado Springs, Colorado. We have recipients currently serving in the U.S. Navy, the U.S. Air Force, and the U.S. Marines. One of our recipients has accepted a job offer with Boeing. Other recipients are working on additional flight ratings for commercial flying, as well as training to be certified training instructors.

After September 11, 2001, it took two years before I was able to sleep with the lights off. It would be three more years before I could remove my wedding band. The panic attacks have lessened over time, and after receiving EMDR treatment, I have been able to slowly wean myself off the antidepressants I had been taking for almost six years. Ten years later, LeRoy's voice is still on the answering machine and his bathrobe still hangs on a hook in the closet.

The years have taken on predictable peaks and valleys. I still have a difficult time with certain days of the year: our wedding anniversary, LeRoy's birthday, Valentine's Day (the day LeRoy proposed), September 11, Christmas, and New Year's Eve. Winters continue to be difficult, as are the first nice days of spring. Ellen and I have talked about how we miss our guys when we see people walking, holding hands, and enjoying the warm weather. After the initial melancholy, spring and summer are usually good months when I feel most like myself, my old self. My voice no longer shakes when I speak.

Most of the people who knew us as a couple do not ask me why I'm not dating. I think they realize how special LeRoy was, how exceptional our relationship was. I would like to imagine that a bond like this can happen more than once in a lifetime. But having that bond, the connection we had, seems to be the exception and not the rule. My friend Dianne, who lost her husband in 2004 when she was thirty-eight years old, says it best: "If I ever get married again, I want a pre-nup that says I get to die first." The thought of growing old alone is not an easy one. When I see someone who is single and happy, content to be alone, I wonder how I can achieve that. I want to know their secret. The need to feel connected still persists.

I bought a wooden sign a few years ago that sits on a shelf in my office. It reads: "God has put me on this earth to do a few things. I'm so far behind I'll never die." I hope to one day learn how to relax again. I am always in constant motion, in part because I'm a single parent to two small children, and there is no shortage of things to be done; but partly because no one is around to tell me to relax. LeRoy saw the Type A part of my personality, and would make me stop when he saw that I needed to. Now no one is here to tell me when to stop, so I keep going.

I have decided to leave New Jersey. The support system I thought I would have is no longer here. I think I want to find my safe place, the place I imagined in my head. A house near the water. Close enough to the ocean that I can hear the waves. For a long time I thought that if I left New Jersey, my memories of LeRoy and our life together would fade, but I now know that that will not happen. The memories will go wherever we go.

I continue to feel ignored by United Airlines. I assume the reality is that two United airplanes crashed that day, and they want people to forget. The LeRoy W. Homer, Jr. Foundation asked to have a small ad featured in *Hemispheres*, the United Airlines inflight magazine. But that went nowhere. Support does however continue to come from ALPA's representatives and their pilot members, as well as the flight attendant groups, who not only publicize and support the causes founded by me, Ellen, and Sandy, but come out in uniform to Shanksville, New York, the Pentagon, and the Garden of Reflection in Pennsylvania on the anniversaries to remind us that they haven't forgotten us. My hope is that United Airlines realizes that taking a tragedy and turning it into something positive is something worthy of their support.

I still believe in God, a God that doesn't make

mistakes, a God that chose my husband to sacrifice his life to save the lives of others. This was what his life's mission was. The question I used to ask myself at my lowest moments—Would it have better if LeRoy and I had never met?—is not one I have to ask anymore. And as much as I still feel the pain of him being taken away from me, my faith gives me the certainty that one day I will see LeRoy again.

I have a difficult time praying for a future for myself, because I have a hard time imagining what it will look like. I used to plan for the long term, but now it's hard to see too far ahead. Raising my children is what guides me in my day-to-day life. The LeRoy W. Homer Jr., Foundation helps me feel that a part of LeRoy is still with us all. Aside from that I'm hopeful there is a better future ahead for me. I was happy once, I would like to be happy again. Looking back, I couldn't have imagined I would make it this far. My life journey continues.

ACKNOWLEDGMENTS

Thanks to my parents, Ena and Waldron Thorpe. I have always felt blessed to be your daughter. To my sister, Heather Thorpe, for her legal expertise, and my brother, Brodrick Thorpe, for keeping me motivated during the many years it took me to write this book.

I am grateful for the encouragement of my BFFs. Pam Newport, we've been friends since elementary school, and even though we have lived in two different countries for most of our adult lives, I always feel you are close. Dawn Roy, you still give me the best "laugh out loud" moments even in the worst of times. Jane Oswari, "you get me, you really get me." And to Digna Yeregui, where do I start? You made me part of your family and helped me survive many difficult days.

Ellen "I wish we'd never met" Saracini, still, almost ten years later, you are there. Sandy Dahl, our husbands were a team, and so are we. Greg Downs, your unfaltering support since the day my life changed forever is something I appreciate more than words can say.

Thanks to John Willig for believing in my project; editors Beth Bruno and Kate Ankofski, for taking what I wrote and making it brilliant; and Deb Lengyel, a great graphic artist, who has become a friend. Thank you to Jennifer Grocki, who was brave enough to read my first draft. Thank you to the United States Air Force Academy for use of the missing man formation photo on the cover.

INDEX

ABOUT THE AUTHOR

Melodie Homer is the widow of First Officer LeRoy Homer. She is the president of the LeRoy W. Homer, Jr. Foundation, an organization that supports and encourages young adults who want to pursue aviation careers. Melodie resides in New Jersey with her two children. All proceeds from sales of this book will fund the LeRoy W. Homer, Jr. Foundation.

SOURCES

Gilbert, M. (2002, October). 9/11 One year later: Victims and survivors grieve, remember and raise pointed questions. *Ebony Magazine*.

Hartocllis, A. (2007, September 4). Little-noticed 9/11 lawsuits will go to trial. *The New York Times*.

Hrywna, M. (2007, February 1). Beamer struggling with missions. *The NonProfit Times*.

Hunt, T. A. (2008, May 1). *News*. Retrieved May 1, 2008, from Comcast: http://www.comcast.net/news.

Meek, J. G. (2004, July 6). 9/11 Cockpits got crisis warnings. *The Washington Daily News*.

Sanderson, B. (2004, July 23). 9/11 Terror: The surprise twist in the saga of Flight 93. *The New York Post*.

Schmeltzer, J. (2002, March 28). $5.7 Million in severance for UAL's Goodwin. *Chicago Tribune*.

Sheehy, G. (2003, August 25). Four 9/11 Moms battle Bush. *The New York Observer*.

Sheehy, G. (2004, February 15). Stewards ID'd hijackers: Early transcripts show. *The New York Observer*.

Smith, P. (2006, May 12). *Ask the Pilot*. Retrieved March 6, 2008, from Salon: http://www.salon.com/tech/col/smith/2006/05/12/askthepilot185/print.html.

Soltis, A. (2004, July 23). Clinton received red flag on hijackings in '98. *The New York Post*.

Todd M. Beamer Foundation. (2002, February). Retrieved May 5, 2008, from HelpAmerica Foundation: http://www.helpamericanfoundation.org/GrantRecipients/toddbeamer.htm.

United Airlines Flight 93: Cockpit voice recorder transcript. (2001, September 11). Shanksville, PA, USA: United States Department of Justice.